A BOOK OF
CURIOUS ADVICE

THE MOST UNUSUAL

MANNERS · MORALS · MEDICINE

FROM DAYS OF YORE

Edited by

RUTH PEPPER SUMMERS

Sterling Publishing, New York

PUBLISHER'S NOTE

The recipes and medical remedies in this book are from the eighteenth and nineteenth centuries, and contain ingredients and recommendations that could be harmful to the modern reader. Please do not attempt to replicate any of these recipes or remedies at home.

Published by Sterling Publishing Co., Inc.
387 Park Avenue South, New York, NY 10016

© 2004 by Ruth Pepper Summers

Distributed in Canada by Sterling Publishing
c/o Canadian Manda Group, 165 Dufferin Street
Toronto, Ontario, Canada M6K 3H6

Distributed in Great Britain by Chrysalis Books
64 Brewery Road, London N7 9NT, England

Distributed in Australia by Capricorn Link
(Australia) Pty. Ltd.
P.O. Box 704, Windsor, NSW 2756, Australia

1-4027-2810-7

Library of Congress Cataloging-in-Publication Data

1 3 5 7 9 8 6 4 2

Manufactured in the United States of America

DEDICATED *to the*
MEMORY *of my* BEST FRIEND,
JOAN MARY PEARCE
(1926 — 2000)

TABLE *of* CONTENTS

ACKNOWLEDGMENTS

THANKS TO THE LOVE OF MY LIFE, MY HUSBAND, BERNARD, for sharing in the joys and disappointments and for the countless cups of coffee delivered to the computer room.

Thanks for the encouragement from my children and grandchildren: Barbara, for her love and interest in searching out research books and sending them over the thousands of miles that separate us; her husband, Ian Soutar; Mark, without whom this book would never have seen the light of day; Shawn Summers; Andy and Justine Summers and Paul Summers, Allison,

Polly and Angel Summers, Meghan Soutar and Sienna Summers. With special thanks to my grandson Stephen Summers, who was honestly interested and laughed in all the right places. Last, but not least, to Renee Joly—only she and I are fully aware of how much day-to-day tangible help she cheerfully gave to me.

Grateful thanks to the Joe Spieler Literary Agency of New York, and to Mr. Spieler for picking me up and to Deirdre Mullane for dusting me off. Thanks also to Sui Mon Wu and my eagle-eyed editor, Beth Tripmacher. Their faith in the success of this book and their helpful suggestions made it all happen.

My thanks and sincere gratitude to my good friends Colleen and Gordon Schottlander, the most generous people I know. To the late Anne Russell, to Ron and Anne Ellerbeck,

Elizabeth Doherty, Mick and Christine Yates, Robin and Zoe Barnes, Isobel Homorodean, and Anne Roper for their generosity in loaning or giving me source books.

I am grateful to Shirley and Diane Brady for their enthusiasm and advice. Special thanks to Richard Bachmann and Jane Irwin of The Different Drummer Bookshop in Burlington for their time, help, and encouragement and to fellow-authors David Creighton, Kim Echlin, and Linwood Barclay for their advice and suggestions.

I am especially indebted to my good friends, Greta and Des Brady, and their delightful secondhand bookshop, Pickwick Books, in Waterdown, Ontario.

INTRODUCTION

MY INTEREST IN BIZARRE ADVICE was first whetted when I borrowed a copy of *Mrs. Beeton's Book of Household Management* and, leafing through the back pages, came across a cure for syphilis in which the patient was advised that a "trip to the seaside might be beneficial." Say what?

I started haunting secondhand bookshops and soon found more delightful titles of the same nature from the eighteenth and early nineteenth centuries. By now I've gathered almost three thousand strange and bizarre "tips" in my sojourn among antique cookbooks, almanacs, and medical manuals, and have chosen just a few to share with you.

Please don't even *think* of trying any of these bizarre and dubious cures in your home today. Many are dangerous and deadly, to say nothing of impractical. Genuine doctors were pretty thin on the ground in those times, and there were no prerequisites for medical training. Anyone could hang out a shingle or write a book that was relied upon by the innocent folk of the time. The printed word was taken as the gospel truth.

Just as an example, look at "How to Cure a Broken Limb" *(p. 27)* by Charles Darwin. Such a messy "cure" would leave the patient minus two pets and dripping with blood and gore. A cut-down broomstick was the only splint that could conveniently be bound on a broken leg; still, it was heaps better than sacrificing those poor puppies for the patient's fleeting benefit.

Old wives and their tales had a place in the past, but, the birthing of babies was strictly a male-dominated field, and the theories these males expounded were sheer nonsense. If a woman suffered a miscarriage, it was her own fault for not "bracing herself" against "outside influences" *(p.49)*. Women turned to the doctors of the times and asked for advice on limiting their families, followed the advice given, and then wondered why they were pregnant again.

Doctors and clergymen were especially eager to give their counsel to young gentlemen and ladies of the time. As you'll note in these pages, they prescribed poisonous remedies for gray hair *(p. 119)* and baldness *(p. 118)*, yet they wouldn't countenance the blush of rouge on a young lady's lips or cheeks, or high heels *(p. 103)*. Why, they asked, would a girl want to appear taller?

Apart from the health and beauty tips, the household "hints" gathered here are of interest to anyone wishing to learn the basics of housekeeping of that time. Homemade mattresses, frozen pumps in winter, hearths in which the fire had died and all this drudgery to be coped with between dawn and dusk because one couldn't consistently afford candles or lamp oil to extend the light of day.

Of necessity, the housewife made use of absolutely everything that ripened: strange fruits, weeds, and animals—such as frogs *(p. 176)*, squirrels *(p. 179)*, and rattlesnakes *(p. 177)*—we wouldn't dream of eating today. It was sheer survival, and no fussy eaters were allowed. Vegetables were considered un- wholesome *(p. 157)*, and fruit was downright dangerous *(p. 148)*.

I hope you enjoy this compilation because I've had a wonderful time putting it together. I'm forever hugging myself with glee and feel- ing quite smug about my secret life as I hurry back to my books, curl up beside the blazing fireplace, and thoroughly put myself in the mood of the past by sipping on a hot rum toddy:

Hot Rum Toddy: Seethe fresh spring water on thy hob and draw a measure of New England Rum from thy firkin. Pour thy water and thy rum into a flip glass or jug and add treacle, honey or Puerto Rico sugar pounded fine. Into thine mixture stir a knob of butter the size of a walnut and a few raspings of nutmeg. Enjoy!

—RUTH PEPPER SUMMERS

BURLINGTON, ONTARIO, OCTOBER 2004

"ASTHMA

IS

CURED BY

THE USE OF

CIGARETTES"

AND OTHER

MYSTERIOUS MALADIES

AND

CURIOUS CURES

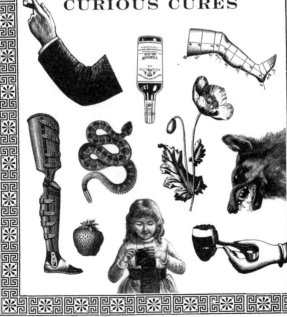

ACORNS *to* CURE ALCOHOL-INDUCED DISEASES

Dr. Burnett strongly commends a "distilled spirit of acorns" as an antidote to the effect of alcohol, where the spleen and kidneys have already suffered, with induced dropsy. It acts on the principle of similars, ten drops being given three times a day in water.

HERBAL SIMPLES, 1914

CURE *for* STUTTERING

Let him who stammers, stamp his foot on the ground at the same time that he utters each syllable and stammering is impossible.

FUN BETTER THAN PHYSIC, 1877

STAMMERING

Stammering is sometimes the result of habit or carelessness; at others it succeeds a long attack of sickness. It is a kind of St. Vitus's Dance of the tongue. . . . Some twenty years ago the New York world was struck with dumb amazement at the instantaneous remedy for stammering, which was, thrusting a knitting-needle through the tongue. But it cured only until the tongue got well, because, while the tongue was sore from the barbarous operation, the extra nervous energy was expended in the instinctive effort to refrain from any other than a careful movement of the tongue.

THE GUIDE BOARD TO HEALTH, PEACE AND COMPETENCE, 1869

Ed. Note: I don't know how long this remedy was tested but I'm sure the onions would give you nightmares—and what about consideration for your bed-partner? Only garlic could be worse!

SIMPLE REMEDY
for
SLEEPLESSNESS

For those troubled with sleeplessness from literary labor or other disturbances of the nervous system, a writer of experience says "just before retiring eat 2 or 3 small raw onions with a little bread, lightly spread with fresh butter, which will produce the desired effect, saving the stupefying action of drugs."

DR. CHASE'S RECIPES, c. 1884

Ed. Note: I was quite amazed to see this "cure" for diabetes mentioned in a book from 1852; this was the only time I came across this condition in all my medical research tomes prior to 1900.

DIABETES

Take of loaf sugar, rosin and alum, equal parts; and take as much as the point of a penknife will contain three times a day; or, steep one ounce of ginger in one pint of good wine and drink two or three glasses a day; or, dissolve in one quart of proof brandy, one ounce of spruce gum and half an ounce of ginger. Dose: from one tablespoonful to half a wineglassful three times a day.

LADIES' INDISPENSABLE
ASSISTANT, 1852

Eating heartily in an exhausted, or even in a greatly debilitated bodily condition is dangerous at any hour. Many a man has fallen apoplectic at the close of a hearty dinner; but the danger is greatly increased by going to bed soon after; for the weight of the meal—a pound or two—resting steadily on the great veins of the body, arrests the flow of the blood. Eating a hearty meal at the close of the day is like giving a laboring man a full day's work to do just as night sets in, although he has been toiling all day.

THE GUIDE BOARD TO HEALTH, PEACE AND COMPETENCE, 1869

To
RESTORE
FROM STROKE
of
LIGHTNING

Shower with cold water for two hours; if the patient does not show signs of life, put salt in the water and continue to shower an hour longer.

THE CANADIAN HOME
COOK BOOK, 1877

ASTHMA

Various substances, smoked or inhaled frequently, have the power of relieving a fit of asthma. Among the most homely of these is the smoke of burnt nitre paper, that is of brown paper dipped in a strong solution of saltpetre and dried. The smoke of this burnt paper often relieves the asthmatic attack. So does a pipe of tobacco, especially in those not accustomed to it. Medicated cigars, too, are prepared for these attacks.

CASSELL'S HOUSEHOLD
GUIDE, C. 1880

CURE for RABIES

When bitten by a supposed mad dog, the only certain remedy is cauterisation, which never fails. It may be applied hours or even days after the wound; indeed, many think that any time previous to the development of the secondary symptoms is efficacious. The cautery may be either actual as applied by hot iron (the hotter it is the less pain, though of course the best is bad) or the galvanic battery, or when the patient's courage is not equal to either, by cutting a stick of lunar caustic to a pencil point and thoroughly working it about in the wound till every point has been well treated. Excision is effectual if done immediately but requires more nerve than most people possess, as it must usually be done by the sufferer himself.

CASSELL'S HOUSEHOLD
GUIDE, C. 1880

RATTLESNAKE BITE

As this book may fall into the hands of those who cannot speedily obtain a physician, it is worth while to mention what is best to be done for the bite of a rattlesnake—Cut the flesh out, around the bite, instantly that the poison may not have time to circulate in the blood. If caustic is at hand, put it upon the raw flesh; if not, the next best thing is to fill the wound with salt, renewing it occasionally. Take a dose of sweet oil and spirits of turpentine to defend

the stomach. If the whole limb swells, bathe it in salt and vinegar freely. It is well to physic the system thoroughly before returning to the usual diet.

THE AMERICAN FRUGAL
HOUSEWIFE, 1832

EAR-WAX *to*
CURE WOUNDS
and
CHAPPED LIPS

Nothing is better than ear-wax to prevent the painful effects resulting from a wound by a nail, skewer, etc. It should be put on as soon as possible. Those who are troubled with cracked lips have found this remedy successful when others have failed.

THE AMERICAN FRUGAL
HOUSEWIFE, 1832

One very popular fruit
that is grown almost all over the
world is strawberries. At various
times in history this fruit has been
used to cure gout and tuberculosis.
The leaves have been used to make
gargles and mouthwashes for sore
throats. There was also a superstition
that you would die if you had a
wound in the head and then ate
strawberries! Doctors of the past
decreed that there was no actual
nutrition to be had from strawberries, but if you served them with
cream, then some nutritional benefit
would be obtained.

There was a strange remedy in
the old days wherein you gathered
strawberries and put them into a
closed glass vessel, and set it in a bed
of hot horse manure for twelve or
fourteen days. Carefully distilled, ☞

the water obtained could be used as a wash for hot inflammations of the eyes.

In France, in days gone by, crushed strawberries were recommended to remove freckles. Some doctors believed the seeds were harmful and advised people to suck their strawberries through a piece of muslin, thereby straining out the seeds. With modern refrigerated transport, we are lucky to have this succulent fruit available to us all through the year.

Tennis is such violent exercise that one cannot recommend women to make use of it, except with a good deal of caution.

Golf has the advantage of keeping its votaries much in the open air, without greatly fatiguing them. Some of the postures are very ugly, it must be confessed. The woman golfer may find it necessary to stand with her feet apart when addressing the ball, but she should be careful not to do so away from the links. It is an extremely ugly and unfeminine attitude.

SOCIAL CUSTOMS, 1911

Ed. Note: Just a little note about "bleeding"—leeches were commonly used by both physicians and householders. Young farm girls earned a few pennies by catching leeches in rivers and streams. They would bundle up their long skirts and wade barefoot up to their knees, using their feet and legs as bait. Then they would pick off the leeches, put them in a little barrel of water, and sell them to the village doctor. Leeches seemed to be in common use as a home remedy also. Well-off households would usually keep a supply on hand.

BLEEDING *a* PATIENT

When a person is bled, he should always be in the standing, or at any rate in the sitting, position for if, as is often the case, he should happen to faint, he can easily be brought to again by the operator placing him flat on his back and stopping the bleeding. It has been recommended, for what supposed advantages we don't know, to bleed people when they are lying down. Should a person, under these circumstances, faint, what could be done to bring him to again? He is laying down already and cannot be placed lower than at present —except, as is most likely to be the case, under ground.

MRS. BEETON'S BOOK OF
HOUSEHOLD MANAGEMENT, 1861

THE LEAST MORTALITY is during the mid-day hours, namely, from ten to three o'clock; the greatest, during early morning hours, from three to six o'clock.

THE GUIDE BOARD TO
HEALTH, PEACE AND
COMPETENCE, 1869

For
DIM EYES

If full of Rheum, or you fear a Pearl or webb is growing therein; take the Yolk out of an Hen's egg, and fill up the Place with the juice of Housteek, and set the Shell on hot Coals to simmer a good while, it being covered; then put the clear into a small Glass-Bottle, put a Drop thereof to the Eye every Night; Or use the distilled Water of Half-Moon Grass, continue the Use of this some Months and to the contrary Wrist apply Hemlock and Salt, and take the Purge.

THE YOUNG MAN'S COMPANION, 1775

Ed. Note: The plague of our schoolchildren today, lice were even more common in days gone by. This remedy makes a virtual incendiary bomb of the victim when you consider that all lighting was by open kerosene, coal oil lamps, or candles! To say nothing of having to cook over open fires!

HEAD LICE

Soak the hair with ordinary kerosene oil for 24 hours, fresh oil being added 3 times during that period; the head in the meantime is to be bound up, to keep in the volatile gases which thereby penetrate the nits. At the end of 24 hours the scalp should be thoroughly washed with soap and water and the lice will all be dead.

MRS. BEETON'S BOOK
OF HOUSEHOLD
MANAGEMENT, C. 1900

Ed. Note: You will notice the use of opium in this next remedy. It, and laudanum (syrup of poppies), was very widely used. It would appear that almost every household had a stock in hand. If they didn't then they just popped down to the local grocery store or druggist. It was sold as a rich, brown, solid cake, sometimes with bits of poppy leaves still in it. It was mostly sold in the form of pills or little sticks. Opium was incredibly cheap; in Britain in the

1800s, you could buy one ounce for a penny. It is reckoned that in the Manchester area five out of six families were regular users, including babies, toddlers, and the adults. Obviously it was easy to obtain or it wouldn't have been advised so frequently for major and minor ailments.

TOOTHACHE,
to Cure so It Will Never Ache again

If the following is the fact, it is the best of all the cures. Dissolve a piece of opium, the size of a small pea, in spirits of turpentine, $\frac{1}{2}$ teaspoonful. Put in the hollow of the tooth upon cotton. It does not stop the pain at once, says the writer, but, if well applied,—the cotton saturated and frequently changed—will soon cause it to never trouble again.

DR. CHASE'S RECIPES, C. 1884

I T IS A GREAT MISTAKE TO THINK THAT A MORNING WALK, OR OTHER FORM OF EXERCISE BEFORE BREAK-FAST, IS HEALTHFUL. A person will remind me that the early air of a summer's morning seems so balmy and refreshing, so cool and delightful, that it cannot be otherwise than healthful. That is begging the question; it is a statement known by scientific observers to be not simply untrue, but to be absolutely false.

THE GUIDE BOARD TO
HEALTH, PEACE AND
COMPETENCE, 1869

MELANCHOLY

Eat often of Cream of Tartar mixt with honey or treacle and shun all Musick Meetings.

THE YOUNG MAN'S COMPANION, 1775

Ed. Note: It is interesting to note that depression was being diagnosed in the 1700s. In the next century physicians concentrated on experimenting with cocaine to treat melancholy. Dr. James Parkinson, who first identified the disease named for him, was instrumental in improving conditions in madhouses and was an eager crusader for the legal protection of the inmates and their families.

To
CURE MADNESS

Hold him under water until he is almost drown'd, then put him to bed in a dark room and his diet only milk pottage, half water.

THE YOUNG MAN'S COMPANION, 1775

Ed. Note: Most people know that the word "bedlam" is derived from the name "Bethlehem" as in the Bethlehem Hospital for the Insane in London, England. The Priory of St. Mary of Bethlehem was used to found this hospital in 1247. The name was almost immediately shortened and corrupted into the word "bedlam" by the locals. By the time of Henry VIII it was firmly established as a lunatic asylum. The mental hospital later moved to Southwark. The old priory is now located under the Liverpool St. Railway Station in London.

CURE *for* JAUNDICE

Fill a quart bottle a third full of chipped inner cherry bark. Add a large teaspoonful soda and fill the bottle with whiskey or brandy. Take as large a dose three times a day as the system will tolerate. If it affects the head unpleasantly, lessen the quantity of bark.

HOUSEKEEPING IN OLD
VIRGINIA, 1879

IF YOU'VE
CUT YOURSELF

Varnish with common furniture varnish. This remedy has been known to prove very efficacious.

HOUSEKEEPING IN OLD
VIRGINIA, 1879

HAVE YOU A FAMILY? If you have not, you need not take any exercise, and you can eat and stuff and guzzle all day, for you are of no account and the sooner you die off and make room for a better man, the better for society at large.

THE GUIDE BOARD TO HEALTH,
PEACE AND COMPETENCE,
1869

To STOP THE FLOW *of* BLOOD

Bind the cut with cobwebs and brown sugar, pressed on like lint. Or, if you cannot procure these, with the fine dust of tea. When the blood ceases to flow, apply laudanum.

COMMON SENSE IN THE
HOUSEHOLD, 1871

HOW *to* CURE *a* BROKEN LIMB

Kill and cut open two puppies and bind them on each side of a broken limb.

DIARIES OF CHARLES DARWIN,
WRITTEN IN SANTA FE,
MEXICO, 1833

PALSY

Caused by compression of a nerve in its origin or course; certain narcotics taken internally; exhalations from lead and arsenic in their preparations; excessive venery, old age, etc.

Symptoms: A loss of sensation or ability of motion in the part affected, which is sometimes one half of the patient, as the right side, or from the hips downwards; at other times only a small part is affected, as the hand, the arm, the leg.

Cure—Electricity should be the first application: the patient should have his face sprinkled with cold water and his hands, arms and legs rubbed in the direction of the circulation—that is, toward the heart. Hartshorn should be applied to the nose and temples and twenty or thirty drops given internally. As soon as the patient begins to recover, a little good wine should be given him.

THE EXPERIENCED
BOTANIST OR INDIAN
PHYSICIAN, 1840

Let not your breast touch
the table or desk on which you
write, for leaning the breast hard against
the edge of the table hath brought many
young men into a consumption.

THE YOUNG MAN'S
COMPANION, 1775

DIPHTHERIA

Diphtheria is now a familiar household word; until within a very few years, indeed, it had never been heard of by one in a million of the masses.

As chemistry has been unable to detect any poisonous ingredient in the atmosphere where diphtheria prevails, we are left to the inference that the air of such a locality is simply deprived of one of its essential health-ingredients. Children are almost exclusively attacked with diphtheria because it is a disease of debility—a disease which depresses every power of life; hence the weaker the subject, the more liable to an attack. The few grown persons who have diphtheria have invariably some scrofulous or other weakening element. Neither a man nor a child, in really vigorous health, is ever attacked with it. There is no evidence whatever that diphtheria is "catching."

THE GUIDE BOARD TO HEALTH,
PEACE AND COMPETENCE, 1869

SEXUAL ORGANS
of MEN

Carry your sexual organs towards the left thigh, where Nature makes the largest place for them.

CREATIVE AND SEXUAL
SCIENCE, 1876

Ed. Note: Do note the astonishing amount of hard liquor in this next remedy. Grandma would be quite squiffy each and every day if she followed this prescription!

MRS. CHASE'S MAGIC TONIC BITTERS *for* WEAK *and* DEBILITATED FEMALES

4 ounces each of best red Peruvian bark, prickly ash bark and poplar root bark. 1 ounce cinnamon bark, ½ ounce cloves. 2 quarts each of whiskey and clear worked cider. Grind all coarsely or bruise with a hammer and put into the jug with the spirits. Shake it up daily for 10 days and take out the dregs and strain. Take a wine-glass of it immediately after each meal.

DR. CHASE'S RECIPES, C. 1884

Leprosy is owing in large part to want of personal cleanliness, and that, terrible as it is, it is the deserved curse of the more than beastly filthiness in which the wretched creatures wallow.

THE GUIDE BOARD TO
HEALTH, PEACE AND
COMPETENCE, 1869

Ed. Note: The mystery of the ages—how to cure the common cold.

COMMON COLD, General Washington's Own Cure

General George Washington gave the following recipe for a cold to an old lady now living in Newport, when she was a very young girl in 1781. He was lodged in her father's house, the old Vernon mansion. As she was being sent to bed early with a very bad cold he remarked to Mrs. Vernon, "my own remedy, my dear madam, is always to eat, just before I step into bed, a hot roasted onion if I have a cold." It may be taken for granted that this simple remedy will be found very efficacious and, if the cold is of recent taking, with the help of either toasting the feet before the fire or stove through the evening, otherwise soaking them in hot water

for 15 to 20 minutes before going to bed, it will be the more likely to succeed. If a hot roasted onion was eaten two or three times during the day it would also help the cure.

DR. CHASE'S RECIPES,
c. 1884

Ed. Note: It is astonishing how many times onions are mentioned as cures for the common cold. I wonder if the strong vapors just opened up all the mucous membranes? Onions were plentiful year round and it would be a poor house, indeed, where an onion wasn't available.

DEAFNESS

If the wax in the ear be hard, then have the oil of bitter almonds dropp'd therein, and a week after let it be syring'd with warm water and beer, but if the wax in the ear be very thin then put in a tent dipped in Melilot Plaister and take sneezing powder often, being warm in bed.

THE YOUNG MAN'S
COMPANION, 1775

Laudanum was syrup of poppies, made by combining opium with alcohol. It was sold under various names, one of which was "Godfrey's Cordial." Every household had a supply on hand to quiet crying infants. Godfrey's Cordial was made by mixing opium with sassafras, brandy, caraway seeds, and treacle or molasses. The sale of opium was completely unregulated both in Britain and the United States up until about 1890. It was sold over the counter with no prescription. Poppies, to supply the large demand, were grown profusely by farmers in New England, and in California, ☞

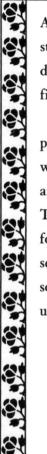

Arizona, Kentucky, and other states. The United States has been described, in the 1800s, as "a dope fiend's paradise."

Many prominent prohibitionists, publicly against the sale of alcohol, were hopelessly addicted to opium and carried it with them at all times. Thomas Jefferson grew poppies for opium on his plantation and the seeds could still be bought at the souvenir shop at the gates right up until 1991.

THE EPILEPTIC HABIT IS NEARLY ALWAYS SET UP IN EARLY CHILDHOOD, the most common causes being terror or sudden fright such as may be occasioned by some sudden noise. When an epileptic attack is repeated two, three or four times there is seldom any refuge short of the grave, the end being fatuity or sudden death. Our greatest anxiety is to attract parental attention to the first attack, so that by exercising a most untiring vigilance against the causes which may repeat it, they may prevent the establishment of the terrible habit for a few years; for, after children enter their teens, the susceptibility of an attack is almost nothing. The cause next in frequency to terror and sudden alarm is connected with the stomach, as eating some unaccustomed or indigestible article of food in large quantities.

Bathing a child in cold water, soon after

a hearty meal, is quite sufficient to bring on an epileptic attack.

Eating largely of soggy bread or of the sodden undercrust of a pie, or of pudding a little soured, may bring on an attack.

It has been said that a black silk handkerchief, thrown over the face while the fit is on, will bring the person "to" instantly. While medicine has no power to cure epilepsy, it is very certain that grown persons can keep it in abeyance by the exercise of a close observation and a sound judgment.

THE GUIDE BOARD
TO HEALTH, PEACE AND
COMPETENCE, 1869

Ed. Note: The listing of ingredients on labels is a very modern concept. In the old days anyone could put anything in a bottle and market it as a magic elixir or cure-all.

COUGH
CANDIES

No cough lozenge is made which does not contain sugar and opium. You may set it down as an infallible fact that no lozenge or cough medicine can be taken even for a short time, without impairing the appetite and causing constipation. I would advise you never to give

or swallow a lozenge or a cough drop as long as you live, unless you wish to be considered a candidate for some lunatic asylum. As for the baby, it likes anything sweet; and they will take the lozenge or the "syrup" from the father's or the mother's hand with such loving, smiling confidence. It is true these things do, in a few weeks, give an unusual brightness of the eye, succeeded by water on the brain on the first attack of sickness and all its growth is in the head and its little body dwindles and its eyes stare out with a maniacal frenzy or an idiotic blankness, closing soon in death.

THE GUIDE BOARD TO
HEALTH, PEACE AND
COMPETENCE, 1869

"A PUPPY
CAN HELP YOU
BREASTFEED"
AND OTHER
PECULIARITIES
OF PREGNANCY
AND
CHILD REARING

A
YOUNG MAN'S
FERTILITY

Previous to the twenty-third year, many a man is incapable of producing healthy children. If he does not destroy his health by premature indulgence, he may destroy his happiness by witnessing his children the prey to debility and deformity.

THE PHYSICAL LIFE
OF WOMAN, 1872

Man HAS A FAR LESS EXQUISITE TENDERNESS FOR HIS OFF-SPRING THAN WOMAN. There is little else than moral sympathy which attaches the father to the infant. Paternal love does not exist save as a thing of growth, of education.

SEXOLOGY, 1904

CAN *the* SEXES BE PRODUCED *at* WILL?

Whenever intercourse has taken place in from two to six days after the cessation of the menses, girls have been produced; and whenever intercourse has taken place in from nine to twelve days after the cessation of the menses, boys have been produced. The wife, therefore, who would wish to bring forth boys only should avoid exposing herself to conception during the first half of the time between her menstrual periods.

THE PHYSICAL LIFE OF WOMAN, 1872

KEEPING CLEAN *during* PREGNANCY

Those who have not been accustomed to bathing should not begin the practice during pregnancy. It is better to preserve cleanliness by sponging with tepid water than by entire baths. Foot baths are always dangerous. Sea-bathing sometimes causes miscarriage. The shower-bath is, of course, too great a shock to the system and a very warm bath is too relaxing. Women of a lymphatic temperament and of a relaxed habit of body are always injured by the bath.

THE PHYSICAL LIFE
OF WOMAN, 1872

Nature makes those handsomest who can have the best children, that they may be selected first and then makes this beauty passion-inspiring to men. Women were created females solely to become mothers.

CREATIVE AND SEXUAL SCIENCE, 1876

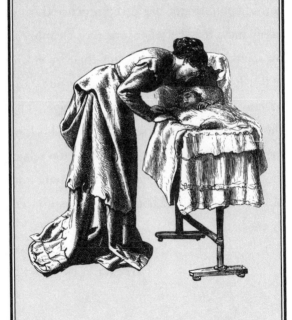

HOW *to* HAVE BEAUTIFUL CHILDREN

During pregnancy the mother should often have some painting or engraving representing cheerful and beautiful figures before her eyes, or often contemplate some graceful statue. She should avoid looking at or thinking of ugly people or those marked with disfiguring diseases.

THE PHYSICAL LIFE OF WOMAN, 1872

To PREVENT MISCARRIAGES

Brace yourself by will-power stoutly against whatever tends to cause it and drink Squaw-vine tea. It is sometimes kept by druggists. The Thompsonian "practice" makes of it a "Mother's Cordial" now kept in some drug-stores for use in pregnancy.

CREATIVE AND SEXUAL SCIENCE, 1876

The BIRTHING CHAMBER

Dr. Elder insists that the confining chamber shall have no artificial heat, even in cold weather, alleging that heat enervates both mother and child.

CREATIVE AND SEXUAL SCIENCE, 1876

ATTENTION *to the* MOTHER *after* CHILDBIRTH

The parts should be gently washed with warm water and a soft sponge or cloth, after which an application of equal parts of claret wine and water will prove pleasant and beneficial. We have also found the anointing of the external and internal parts with goose grease to be very soothing and efficient in speedily allaying all irritation. This ought all to be done under cover to guard against the taking of cold.

And:

The patient should maintain rigidly the recumbent position for the first few days, not raising her shoulder from the pillow for any purpose and should abstain from receiving visitors and from any social conversation for the first twenty-four hours.

And:

After the third or fourth day the dress should be changed.

THE PHYSICAL LIFE
OF WOMAN, 1872

Ed. Note: How terribly unsanitary . . . wearing the same clothing for up to four days after delivering your baby! Over the years the "lying-in" period has become shorter and shorter and today's mother often leaves the hospital within twenty-four hours of giving birth. A new mother is advised to get up and walk very quickly after giving birth; this has saved countless lives by preventing blood clots (embolisms) from forming.

> **J**UST SIX MONTHS AND SEVEN DAYS FROM YOUR LAST MENSES, says Dr. Naegele, will be the true time for labor. CREATIVE AND SEXUAL SCIENCE, 1876

IF YOU DON'T BREAST FEED

Half the spoon-fed infants of New York city die every summer.

CREATIVE AND SEXUAL SCIENCE, 1876

A PUPPY CAN HELP YOU BREAST FEED

Women who have never suckled often experience difficulty in nursing on account of the sunken and flat condition of the nipples. The nipples may be drawn out by a common breast pump, by suction with a tobacco pipe, by the use of the hot-water bottle or by the application of a puppy or of an infant a little older.

THE PHYSICAL LIFE OF WOMAN, 1872

BABY'S BELLY-BAND

The belly-band of an infant should be worn at least four months. It is commonly supposed that the tighter this bandage is drawn the better. This is a mistake; too tight drawing may produce the very rupture it is intended to remedy. A scorched linen rag with fresh mutton tallow on it, or a raisin split open are suitable to apply when the cord drops off.

THE FAMILY NURSE, 1837

Ed. Note: These "belly-bands" were strips of material about a yard long and four to five inches wide. They were tied tightly around the baby's tummy to "support" him or her. Later you might put a "stayed" vest on the baby to support the back and chest. All these measures are completely unnecessary as we know today.

KEEP CHILDREN'S HAIR CUT CLOSE UNTIL TEN OR TWELVE YEARS OLD; IT IS BETTER FOR HEALTH AND THE BEAUTY OF THE HAIR. Do not make children cross-eyed by having hair hang about their foreheads where they see it continually.

THE AMERICAN FRUGAL HOUSEWIFE, 1832

A SYMPTOM of SICKNESS in YOUR CHILD

If a child wakes up in the morning and calls for a drink of water the first thing, such child is perfectly certain to be sick before noon. The course to be pursued is to keep him in bed and, by warm drinks, promote perspiration, eating nothing whatever until the afternoon, when he may amuse himself by nibbling at some cold, dry bread and the next day he will be about again. Otherwise, a breakfast will be eaten, fever comes on, vomiting and several days illness.

FUN BETTER THAN
PHYSIC, 1877

Ed. Note: Referring to "medicine"—they were talking about opium and laudanum, given to ensure a night's sleep for the mother or nurse. A very common procedure in Europe and North America during these years!

MEDICINE

Never give medicine to a very young child. Many have thus lost darling children. It will, if not murdered, be permanently injured. It cries often on account of tight clothes or the pricking of pins. If medicine must be given at all, give it to the nurse.

LADIES' INDISPENSABLE
ASSISTANT, 1852

P ARLIAMENTARY RETURNS SHOW THAT, OF TWENTY-EIGHT HUNDRED INFANTS ANNUALLY SENT TO VARIOUS HOSPITALS TO BE TAKEN CARE OF, TWENTY-FOUR OUT OF TWENTY-FIVE DIED BEFORE THEY WERE A YEAR OLD! A law was immediately passed that they should be sent to the country thereafter, when it was found that only nine of twenty-five died the first year.

This simple, unvarnished statement of an indisputable fact ought to impress the mind of every parent deeply, with the importance and the duty of using all practicable means for securing to children the habitual breathing of the purest air possible.

THE GUIDE BOARD TO
HEALTH, PEACE AND
COMPETENCE, 1869

IRREGULARITY
in the MENSES *in*
ADOLESCENTS

The common causes of irregularity in the menses are taking cold, wet feet, too much mental application, sedentary life, want of exercise, abuse of coffee, stimulants or narcotics, violent exercise, checked perspiration, laziness, late hours, want of attention to the daily evacuations, excitement, anger, passion, grief, worry, immorality, disappointments, home-sickness, mental shocks, frights.

The hygiene of a girl at this critical period should be guarded, both morally and physically. Her mind should be free from cares or sorrows; free from the shackles of society;

not laden with engrossing studies; prevented from reading amorous literature, or too much of romance and novels, guarded from all nervous shocks. Her body should be allowed to develop, untrammeled by unsuitable dress, unimpeded by confinement to the house or school. The open air should be her life, healthy exercise her practice, innocent pleasures her resources.

SEXOLOGY, 1904

SAFETY *for* CHILDREN

Children should be instructed to run with the mouth shut for the first block or two after getting out of doors in cold weather.

THE GUIDE BOARD TO HEALTH,
PEACE AND COMPETENCE, 1869

HORSEBACK EXERCISE CARRIED TO FATIGUE SEEMS OCCASIONALLY TO HAVE CONDUCED TO PREGNANCY.

THE PHYSICAL LIFE OF WOMAN, 1872

HOW *to* VACCINATE YOUR CHILD

If parents are so situated that a doctor cannot be called, they may perform the vaccination without the least risk. If any person in the

vicinity has the kine-pox, obtain the matter by opening one of the pustules with the point of a needle on the eighth or ninth day. Slightly scratch the upper part of the arm or leg in two places so as to bring blood; apply the matter on a little lint and bind it on. It will rarely fail to produce the eruption in three or four days.

THE FAMILY NURSE,

1837

SOME TIME AGO A CHILD DIED UNDER SUCH CIRCUMSTANCES THAT THE PHYSICIAN MADE AN EXAMINATION AFTER DEATH and found that the stomach was ulcerated in various places and that at each ulcerated spot there was a bit of finger nail stuck into the membranes. The symptoms attendant on the pernicious habits of girls at school, particularly of biting off the fingernails, are great paleness of the face and occasional bleeding at the nose. When once a child gets into this habit it is almost impossible to break it up by verbal admonitions or even by punishment; the very fact of its being forbidden seems to impel to the act of biting the nails and swallowing the particles when they are alone or unobserved. A very efficient method of breaking up the habit is to compel the wearing of a woollen mitten.

THE GUIDE BOARD TO HEALTH, PEACE AND COMPETENCE, 1869

Walter Hunt, a mechanic in New York, invented safety pins. He patented the safety pin in 1849. He also built the first sewing machine in the United States but, fearing that it would put too many people out of work, did not pursue the idea. Prior to safety pins, mothers used "swaddling cloths" on their babies, a long strip of soft cloth, which was wrapped around the baby's bottom. As it got wet or soiled it was simply unwound and rearranged so that a dry part of the cloth was where it was needed. Well-organized mothers sewed tapes or strings onto triangular pieces of cloth to use as diapers. Native Americans and many other cultures of the world have also used swamp mosses, such as sphagnum, as diapers in the past. Swamp moss absorbs ☞

up to twenty times its own weight in moisture and neutralizes ammoniac odors, so it was just ideal for diapers!

Diapers got their name from the diagonal or diamond pattern of weave used on linen, cotton, or broadcloth. At first it was only the name for the pattern—then it began to take on the meaning of its end use. No pun intended! It is the most absorbent weave.

Disposable diapers were invented in 1890 but they were very

expensive and not at all like the ones so popular today. The idea did not really catch on until the mid-1960s. There was much controversy about the expense of disposable diapers and you had to weigh your choice. In Britain, terry towelling was commonly used for diapers but heavy gauze cotton was the norm in North America. Every prospective mother would buy about three dozen and sometimes that wasn't enough. It was risky to neglect washing them daily as you could run out of diapers very easily.

Dirty diapers were held securely and flushed with water in the toilet and then stored in a covered bucket in the bathroom. I read, once, about someone in the deep South who had placed a dirty diaper into a plastic bag and then left it in the sun for three days . . . it spontaneously combusted and set a building on fire!

LEFT HAND USE *and* CAUSES THEREOF

Infants carried mainly on the left arm of the nurse very soon get to use the left hand. Whether from this or any other cause, the child is getting to be left-handed, a large woollen mitten, tied to the wrist so that it cannot be easily removed, will break up the habit in a short time.

THE GUIDE BOARD TO HEALTH,
PEACE AND COMPETENCE, 1869

OPIUM *for* BABIES

Do not give opium to children under the age of one year except on the advice of a physician.

THE PRACTICAL HOME
PHYSICIAN, 1892

A NUMBER OF ANCIENT WRITERS HAVE ALLEGED, AND IT HAS BEEN RE-ASSERTED BY MODERN AUTHORITIES, that sleeping on sponge is of service to those who desire to increase their families. Hemlock boughs make a bed which has a well-established reputation for similar virtues.

The odor of cone-bearing trees has a well-known influence upon the fruitfulness of wedlock. Those who live in pine forests have ordinarily large families of children.

THE PHYSICAL LIFE OF WOMAN, 1872

Ed. Note: The "sponge" referred to was not the foam rubber that we know today—plastic or styrofoam had not yet been invented. These mattresses must have been made from genuine sea sponge and would have been extremely expensive.

"DON'T WASH

THE HAIR MORE THAN

ONCE

A

MONTH"

AND OTHER

BEFUDDLING FASHION,

BEAUTY, AND

GROOMING TIPS

Ed. Note: There were no handy roll-up tubes of lipstick in those days. This recipe was probably stored in little containers or in a twist of paper and carried to parties and dances. The first actual lipstick in a metal case, as we know it today, was developed in the United States in 1915.

RED LIP SALVE

Oil of sweet almonds, two ounces; pure olive oil, six ounces; spermaceti, one and one half ounce; white wax, one ounce. Color with carmine and perfume with oil of roses.

HOUSEKEEPING IN OLD
VIRGINIA, 1879

Ed. Note: All sorts of everyday items were used surreptitiously as rouge or blush when a young lady was off to a party or ball—she might redden her cheeks and lips with beet juice, strawberries, or diluted cochineal. Cochineal is the source of carmine, a deep red dye, and it is obtained from the plant lice of the prickly pear cactus that grows in Peru.

POISONING
from COSMETICS

The most common sources of poisoning are from powders for the face and dyes for the hair. The most frequent poison in these articles is lead. Hair dyes sometimes contain other poisonous substances as well. Those who insist upon being certain of the harmlessness of their toilet articles can use the following mixture which can be put up at any drug store.

A white powder for the face can be made as follows: Wheat Starch, 220 parts, Oxide of Zinc, 30 parts, Oil of Rose, four drops.

THE PRACTICAL HOME
PHYSICIAN, 1892

Ed. Note: I believe the "flake white" referred to in this hint is none other than the extremely toxic white lead.

COSMETICS *for* *the* FACE

For a very fine one, try Mrs. Chase's following treatment for pimpled face, etc. Put flake white, $1/2$ ounce in bay rum and water, each 2 ounces and applied after shaking, to the face, with a piece of soft flannel and when dry, wiped or rubbed off where too much white shows, is excellent.

DR. CHASE'S RECIPES,
c. 1884

WRINKLES

The best way to prevent wrinkles is to avoid making the same grimaces—raising the forehead in an expression of surprise, knitting the brows as in frowning, half closing the eyes as near-sighted people do—all of which are things which tend to form the same creases in the skin. Gentle massage will remove the wrinkles.

THE GIRL'S OWN ANNUAL,
VOL. XXIV, 1903

Ed. Note: Make of the following what you will, but I've discovered, from reading other medical books of the same era, that people really thought that blackheads and pimples were worms that had embedded themselves in the face. And what kind of a worm was it? One with a black head; thus the name.

FACE WORMS

To remove worms in the face, place over the black spot the hollow end of a watch-key and press firmly.

And:

To guard against face worms and pimples wash your face night and morning in strong cologne water and rub dry with a coarse towel. Also take a thimbleful of sulphur in a glass of milk 2 or 3 times a week before breakfast. Continue the practice a couple of weeks.

DR. CHASE'S RECIPES,
c. 1884

TREATMENT *for a* FLORID FACE

Get some strong lead lotion and moisten a piece of lint with it and sleep with it laid across your nose. Do not wash your face oftener than you need and then, if possible, wash it with milk or salad oil instead of water. Avoid all food which flushes your face.

THE GIRL'S OWN ANNUAL,
VOL. XXIV, 1903

To LIGHTEN YOUR SKIN *and* REMOVE FRECKLES

Horse radish, boiled in milk, is said to be a good wash to remove tan and freckles. The leaves are a good application for rheumatic pains and they often relieve the tooth-ache but, if kept on the face too long, will produce a blister.

THE FAMILY NURSE,
1837

RULES *for* BATHING *as* DRAWN UP *by the* ROYAL HUMANE SOCIETY

In addition to the home or douche bath, there is the plunge bath, river or other, to be considered. Bathing in general, such as we now refer to, is very injudiciously practiced and it is

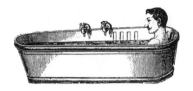

much to be regretted that parents, heads of schools and others, are so extremely ignorant generally of the best rules for bathing.

1. Avoid bathing within two hours after a meal.
2. Avoid bathing when exhausted.
3. Avoid bathing when the body is cooling after perspiration.
4. Bathe when the body is warm.
5. Avoid chilling the body after bathing by sitting naked on banks or in boats.
6. Avoid staying too long in the water. Leave it directly there is the slightest feeling of chilliness.

7. Avoid bathing altogether in the open air if, after having been a short time in the water, there is a sense of chilliness or numbness of hands and feet.

8. The vigorous and strong may bathe early in the morning on an empty stomach.

9. The young and the weak had better bathe three hours after a meal— best after breakfast.

10. Those who are subject to attacks of giddiness and faintness, or palpitations, etc., should not bathe without first consulting their medical adviser.

CASSELL'S HOUSEHOLD
GUIDE, C. 1880

DAILY BATHING

It is my opinion, founded on observation, that a daily bath, to one in good health, is not only not beneficial, but is injurious, while it deprives a man of a valuable prophylactic when he is really sick. A man who is well should let himself alone!

A daily bath, shower or otherwise is a modern invention, devised to sell bath-tubs. I personally have known but two men who acknowledged to a daily shower bath, literally a shower bath, every day. One of them died years ago of chronic diarrhoea, the other was a hydropathist, a great, stout, raw-boned six footer. I sat at the same table with him for many months; he was always bathing and was always sick.

When a man is not well, bathing of some kind is advisable under certain circumstances, but it should not be continued too long; as soon as he is well he ought to stop.

THE GUIDE BOARD TO HEALTH,
PEACE AND COMPETENCE, 1869

As recently as the 1940s there were tenements and apartment buildings in Glasgow, London, and New York that did not have a single bathtub in the whole building forcing the tenants to go to the public baths for their weekly ablutions.

In the early church, baths were thought to be wicked luxuries and a waste of time, an indulgence akin to sinning. A dirty body with a clean soul was more acceptable to God. Later in history, baths were seldom taken for the purpose of cleanliness; they were thought of as "cures." Hot water, prior to the 1900s, was seriously frowned on for bathing. It was reputed to be an unnecessary luxury that weakened the system. Cold baths and showers were thought to be invigorating and bracing. In boarding schools they ☞

were useful tools against the natural sex drives of adolescent boys.

The Romans discovered the therapeutic value of the natural hot springs in the city of Bath *(Aquae Sulis)* in England but, after the Romans left Britain in about A.D. 500, the baths fell into disrepair. They were rediscovered in the ninth century, when Prince Bladud, who was King Lear's father, contracted leprosy. He was banished from the Court and became a swineherd. One day his pigs were wallowing in the water of the springs at Bath, and Bladud decided to wallow with them. It is claimed that his leprosy was immediately cured.

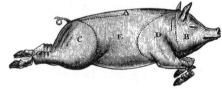

There upon he promptly founded the city of Bath, and there a statue is erected to his memory. The hot springs have been used to treat all sorts of inward and outward ailments: stomach problems, constipation, and heart irregularities were treated by drinking the waters, while rheumatism, arthritis, sciatica, and skin disorders were supposedly cured by bathing in the public pools. Of course this was only available to the wealthy, and the baths became hotbeds of gossip, vice, frivolity, and fashion.

The Black Death, spread by rat fleas, and the plagues of medieval times could not have decimated the population of Europe had people had the means and custom of regular baths. One valid reason for not bathing was the difficulty in obtaining water. The rural population

of the Americas had to resort to carrying water in oaken buckets from streams and lakes, often up to a mile distant. In the growing towns a common well would be sunk at an intersection and most people kept a rain barrel to collect the rainwater from the roof of their house. This rain barrel, often full of mosquito larvae was a source of serious disease.

Soap was made by boiling vats of fat and grease from the kitchens and slaughtered livestock, and made up before it became rancid and smelly. Everyone had a favorite recipe for soap.

Body odors must have been horrendous, even among royalty and the most fashionable people of society. The clothing was cumbersome and difficult to launder, and there seems to have been very little regard for cleanliness. Peasant folk, serfs,

and servants wore the same clothes day and night, year after year. The wealthy had elaborate and voluminous bejeweled gowns that would have been impossible to keep clean and fresh. Food stains, dirt, dust, and perspiration would play havoc with your wardrobe but, then again, everyone was in the same boat.

BATHING

Once a week is often enough for a decent white man to wash himself all over. If a man is a pig in his nature, then no amount of washing will keep him clean, inside or out.

Baths should be taken early in the morning. Any kind of bath is dangerous soon after a meal or soon after fatiguing exercise. No man or woman should take a bath at the close of the day unless by the advice of the family physician. Many a man, in attempting to cheat his doctor out of a fee, has cheated himself out of his life, ay, it is done every day.

The safest mode of a cold bath is a plunge into a river; the safest time is instantly after getting up.

THE GUIDE BOARD TO HEALTH,
PEACE AND COMPETENCE, 1869

DEODORANT

Aqua Ammonia is used by some for the removal of unpleasant personal odors; but it has one of its own scarcely more agreeable and perhaps it acts only by having a stronger smell.

THE GUIDE BOARD TO HEALTH, PEACE AND COMPETENCE, 1869

Ed. Note: Although deodorants were on sale early in the 1900s, they didn't come into general use until about 1945. A few of the first deodorants on the market were "Mum" and "Odorono."

FALLACIES
about the CARE
of the TEETH

The best and safest tooth wash in the world is tepid water. There is not a tooth powder in existence, nor a tooth wash, that does not inflict a physical injury to the teeth and promote their decay. The teeth were never intended to be pearly white. Every intelligent dentist knows that the whiter the teeth are, the sooner and the more certainly they will decay. He also knows that those teeth are the soundest, last the longest and are the most useful, which have a yellowish tint. Then why provide powders to take off this yellowish surface?

FUN BETTER THAN PHYSIC, 1877

Ed. Note: So much for flossing; this doctor highly disapproves of the practice.

MORE *on* DENTISTRY

Many dentists inculcate two most mischievous errors. Threads should never be drawn between the teeth. A permanent tooth ought never to be extracted to make room for others. Nature knows what she is about; every tooth is needed to develop the jaw.

THE GUIDE BOARD TO HEALTH,
PEACE AND COMPETENCE, 1869

To
BEAUTIFY TEETH

Dissolve two ounces of borax in three pints boiling water and before it is cold add one teaspoon of spirits of camphor; bottle it for

use. A teaspoon of this with an equal quantity of tepid water.

THE CANADIAN HOME
COOK BOOK, 1877

Ed. Note: This next hint will make you shudder and set your teeth on edge.

To SWEETEN *the* BREATH

A lump of charcoal held in the mouth two or three times in a week and slowly chewed, has a wonderful power to preserve the teeth and purify the breath. It would not be wise to swallow that or any other gritty substance in large quantities or very frequently; but, once or twice a week a little would be salutary. A bit of charcoal, as big as a cherry, merely held in the mouth a few hours, has a good effect. Those who are troubled with an offensive breath might chew it very often and swallow it but seldom.

THE LADIES VASE
OR POLITE MANUAL FOR
YOUNG LADIES, 1847

Ed. Note: Diets weren't an all-consuming passion in previous centuries—most people were concerned with getting enough food rather than too much. Still, a few problems did exist among the wealthy. Nutrition was not studied in those days and some of the diet notions are bizarre.

WEIGHT PROBLEMS

The women of Senegal expand to an extraordinary degree of plenitude, in the course of a few months only, by gorging themselves with fresh dates. Any woman who is troubled with

 a superfluity of fat and wishes to get rid of it, can succeed by persevering in a certain diet and regimen. She must live in a warm and dry climate, avoid those articles of diet which are especially fat-producing and eat those which are not, with a plentiful supply of acids, lead an active life, with a brisk exercise both of body and mind, lie on a hard bed and never remain on it long.

BAZAR BOOK OF DECORUM, 1877

For
WOMEN WHO WANT
to LOSE WEIGHT

Keep on bearing children as long and often as possible.

CREATIVE AND SEXUAL
SCIENCE, 1876

BALDNESS IS CONSIDERED A GREAT CALAMITY BY MANY. It is brought on, in many cases, by wearing the hat too constantly or by any other means which keeps the head too warm. Another cause of baldness is the filthy practice of keeping the hair soaked in various kinds of grease.

As a hair restorative our readers would do well to try the following wash: Pour three pints of hot water on four handfuls of the stems and leaves of the garden "box"—boil it for fifteen minutes in a closed vessel, then pour it in an earthen jar and let it stand ten hours; next strain the liquid and add three tablespoonfuls of cologne water; wash the head with this every morning. If this wash fails after a few weeks perseverance, the baldness may be considered incurable.

THE GUIDE BOARD TO
HEALTH, PEACE AND
COMPETENCE, 1869

There are very few people in the world whose names have entered the English language; some I can think of offhand are Hoover, Quisling from Norway, Boycott from Ireland, Bloomer from the United States, and the British author of a popular diet scheme, William Banting. Banting's diet became famous throughout the English-speaking world and his name became a household word, synonymous with "dieting." William Banting was born in 1798 and started putting on weight when he was about thirty years old. He asked his doctor friends for advice and was told to exercise more. He lived on a river, and then took up rowing and rowed for about two hours every day. All this expenditure of energy made him ravenous and he ate even more than before.

His weight really bothered him and he found himself huffing and puffing with even the simplest exertion such as tying his shoes. He started checking himself into the hospital and going to spas. This went on for twenty years until, by the time he was sixty-four, he weighed 202 pounds and he was only 5′ 5″ tall. Finally, with the continued advice of his doctor, he devised his own low-carbohydrate diet and was successful at last. On this diet he lost forty-six pounds in the first year. He was so very pleased with himself that he published, at his own expense, a slim booklet entitled "Letter on Corpulence Addressed to the Public." This was published in 1863 and given away for free. His little treatise was pooh-poohed by doctors at the time, mostly because it had been written by a layman, but ☞

the book was a huge success and went into several printings. People following his diet actually did lose weight. Finally, to curb his expenses, he started charging for his book. His famous diet is given below and seems to be the precursor of Dr. Atkin's diet, which is sweeping the world today.

MR. BANTING'S FAMOUS DIET

Breakfast: five to six ounces of either beef, mutton, kidneys, broiled fish, bacon or cold meat of any kind except pork or veal, a large cup of tea or coffee without milk or sugar, a little biscuit or one ounce of dry toast.

Dinner at 2 P.M.: five or six ounces of any fish, except salmon,

herrings or eels, any meat except pork or veal, any vegetable except potato, parsnip, beet root, turnip or carrot, one ounce of dry toast, fruit out of a pudding not sweetened, any kind of poultry or game and two or three glasses of good claret, sherry or madeira.

Tea at 6 P.M.: two or three ounces of cooked fruit, a rusk or two and a cup of tea without milk or sugar.

Supper at 9 P.M.: three or four ounces of meat or fish, similar to dinner, with a glass or two of claret or sherry and water.

THE PRACTICAL HOME
PHYSICIAN, 1892

HAVE YOUR WIFE'S BREASTS DECLINED SINCE YOU COURTED AND MARRIED HER? It is because her womb has declined and rebuilding it will rebuild them and nursing up her love will rebuild both her womb and breasts. Come, court her up again as you used to before marriage and, besides reddening up her now pale cheeks, lightening her now lagging motion, you will redevelop her shrivelled breasts. Stay home of nights from your club rooms, billiard saloons and lodges to read or talk to her or escort her to parties, lectures, concerts and you'll get well paid every time you see her bust.

CREATIVE AND
SEXUAL SCIENCE,
1876

ℐ𝑜
LOSE WEIGHT

To one who is fat, the best cure for it is to eat less and to eat nothing except meat—one or two pounds of meat a day and four glasses of hot water between meals. No bread, butter, potatoes, pudding or anything else.

THE GIRL'S OWN ANNUAL,
VOL. XXIV, 1903

TIGHT-LACING

It is hoped that none of our readers need to be cautioned against tight-lacing, one of the most absurd habits ever suggested by vanity and adopted by ignorance. If they do, we can only repeat what has been urged a thousand times before against the practice, that a small waist is not elegant tested by any of the canons of taste—that if it were it would be purchased at too high a price if it is to be obtained by tight-lacing, which, compressing the most vital parts of the body, pushes the liver out of its place, injures the digestion and frequently deranges the action of the heart; while as it sooner or later causes a red nose, it can scarcely be said to improve the personal appearance of any one who indulges in it.

BEETON'S SIXPENNY COOKERY BOOK FOR THE PEOPLE, c. 1890

TIGHT LACING
of CORSETS

Next time you have a headache, retire to the privacy of your own room and remove your corset. Tight lacing causes palpitations and irregularity of the heart. Tight lacing affects the brain and causes insomnia and causes the hair to fall out in handfuls. Tight lacing causes pimples and skin blotches on the face. It ages and wrinkles a woman long before her time. Nature never intended women to wear corsets, else she would have provided her with an outside shell instead of an inside skeleton. Perfect corsets have yet to come, and come they no doubt will.

THE GIRL'S OWN ANNUAL,
VOL. XXVII, 1907

WEIGHT *of* CLOTHING *and* FASHION

Many women suffer a good deal from the weight of their dress, especially from the common habit of suspending the petticoats round the waist, so that the weight has to be borne on the loins. Under some circumstances, and in certain conditions, this is very injurious and as it admits of a simple remedy, should not be tolerated. A couple of pieces of strong webbing cut of the required length to serve as a pair of braces, should be made to join with a crosspiece to come across the shoulders. These suspenders may fasten to the petticoat with buttons behind and before, or a strong wire hook can easily be made to attach more than one article of dress.

BEETON'S SIXPENNY COOKERY
BOOK FOR THE PEOPLE, C. 1890

HIGH HEELS

The high-stilt heel is ruinous for the feet and is changing the female's gait entirely and a woman can no longer walk, nor can she even do a graceful waddle. She has no more poetry of motion and no more music in her feet than a man with a couple of wooden legs. These high heels are meant to increase the apparent height of the wearer, but is height in a girl really an attraction? I doubt it.

THE GIRL'S OWN ANNUAL,
VOL. XXVII, 1907

OSTRICH FEATHERS

About half the feathers of the ostrich drop out naturally, but we fear some are pulled out, but no great cruelty is used. We do not suppose it hurts the bird very much or for very long.

THE GIRL'S OWN ANNUAL,
VOL. XXVII, 1907

WHAT *a* GIRL
SHOULD WEAR WHILE
OUT HUNTING

If you mean to follow the guns, you will not be permitted to wear any piece of clothing, how-ever charming, of a bright or noticeable color; in fact you must try to do as the grouse does and imitate the color of your surroundings as closely as possible. I therefore advise the pur-chase of one of those delightful hand-knitted jerseys, which are almost rainproof. This jersey is to be worn with a short kilted skirt of heather green hopsack. The hat is a tam-o'shanter of the same color. The jerseys are ideal things to wear over blouses of white silk in treacherous weather.

THE GIRL'S OWN ANNUAL,
VOL. XXIV, 1903

Ed. Note: Fashion and customs certainly have changed; today you'd want to wear something distinguishable and colorful so that you don't get mistaken for a wild animal.

SURGICAL INSTRUMENTS

Surgical instruments are quite the rage nowadays. Men and women as "flat as a flounder" patronize abdominal supporters when the great mischief is that they haven't anything to support.

Deaf women, the dumb ones having all died off before the flood, are provided with patent "auricles" which stick out on each side of the head like two great rams' horns, all regardless of the fact of whether there is any hearing to be aided or not. Then there are shoulder-braces and back-straps, respirators, inhalers, et id omne, ad infinitum; so that there is scarcely a member of the human body that is not pro-vided with an "aid." The stomach has a million; among the worst are German gin and British beer, made out of worse than bilge-water. Now any intelligent physician knows that the vast mass of persons who patronize these great variety of supporters need aids of a very different kind . . . the most valuable general "supporter" and the only one needed in nine cases out of ten is to make the patient go to work and compel him to live on his daily earnings.

THE GUIDE BOARD
TO HEALTH, PEACE AND
COMPETENCE, 1869

We take our unmentionables for granted these days and are inclined to think that they have been in existence forever, but that is not the case at all. Underwear certainly was not sold in stores prior to about 1880. Not even royalty or other gentry wore underwear in days of yore. Dozens of petticoats, yes, but panties and brassieres were nonexistent. Drawers with buttons at the waist began to be fashionable, but only among the wealthy.

The first brassiere was patented in 1884 in Washington, D.C., and it was very much like our modern sports bra. Another brassiere was patented in 1889 in Paris, but bras generally were not worn until about 1925. Corsets have been around for a few centuries and were the only undergarment universally worn in the civilized world. ☞

Petticoats (little coats) were originally worn by men, under their doublets, in the 1500s. For women's wear they were designed to support the voluminous skirts and bustles and crinolines. Crinolines were originally made of horsehair. The word "crin" means "horsehair" in French. In the 1800s some petticoats had a band of steel around the lower hem to keep them rigidly in shape. Your undies could weigh fifteen or

twenty pounds. Imagine the
tedium of hauling that weight
around all day.

Ladies had a terrible time trying
to keep their skirts and petticoats
clean as they waded through the
muddy streets. It was this that started
a big change in the middle of the
1800s, defended by Amelia Bloomer.
Mrs. Bloomer was the editor of the
"Lily"—a temperance paper—and
one day a friend of hers showed up
in a specially-made costume consist-
ing of a startlingly new length of skirt
that came to mid-calf. Under this ☞

skirt was worn a pair of harem-like pants, voluminous and full but tight at the waist and ankles. Seemingly this would solve the problem of petti-coats and skirts getting so filthy.

Mrs. Bloomer thought these were a fine idea. She never invented "bloomers" nor did she ever wear them, but she defended them in her newspaper. This caused a great uproar and newspaper cartoonists caricatured them; preachers banned them from church. They were con-sidered obscene. At least they had broken some ground, but the new fashion was really too radical for the times. It did not catch on to any great extent until the idea was resurrected early in the 1900s in the form of gym bloomers, taking their name from Mrs. Bloomer.

CRIMPS *in* DAMP WEATHER— *To* KEEP HAIR *in* PLACE

A very good bandoline (hair-setting lotion) is made by the use of gum Arabic or gum tragacanth (the Arabic is most use while the tragacanth is the best) say ½ ounce powdered, pouring on just enough boiling water to dissolve it; then adding alcohol enough to make it rather thin. Let stand open all night then bottle for use. Directions: Wet the bangs with this mixture at bed time and twist or curl the bangs upon the forehead as desired; then put over a bit of lace or gauze band to keep it in position till dry, or rather, till morning; then remove the bandeau and pull the crimps out with the fingers until they are soft and fluffy.

DR. CHASE'S RECIPES,
c. 1884

> **S**TRIPES ARE ALREADY BECOMING A WEARINESS TO THE EYE. **If** Dame Fashion had had her way we should all have worn pyjama stripes of the most outre type this season. It is the exaggeration of a fashion when it is a little marked which kills it. Stripes will die a sudden death.
>
> THE GIRL'S OWN ANNUAL,
> VOL. XXVII, 1907

SHAMPOOING

Daily washing of the hair is very bad for it. Women should not wash their hair oftener than once in three weeks. For washing the hair the best thing to use is a little quilla bark and hot water.

THE GIRL'S OWN ANNUAL,
VOL. XXIV, 1903

Ed. Note: Quilla bark is obtained from a tree native to South America—sometimes called "soapbark."

BEAUTY TIPS
from a DOCTOR

Don't wash the hair more than once a month. Do not use soap, but the yolk of a new-laid egg in rain or river water. Don't roast the head and hair in the sun.

Excitement, if continued day after day and night after night, is destructive to the hair. So are hot rooms and the blaze of electric lights.

THE GIRL'S OWN ANNUAL,
VOL. XXVII, 1907

Ed. Note: A word to the wise: I've known girls who've shampooed their hair with raw eggs and then tried to rinse it out with hot water . . . instant hard-boiled eggs.

HEALTHY HAIR

New England rum, constantly used to wash the hair, keeps it very clean and free from disease and promotes its growth a great deal more than Macassar oil. Brandy is very strengthening to the roots of the hair but it has a hot, drying tendency which New England rum has not.

THE AMERICAN FRUGAL
HOUSEWIFE, 1832

Ed. Note: Macassar is a hair dressing from the island of Macassar, its name eventually meaning any exotic oil from the East. Those special mats sewn or crocheted for the backs of sofas, chesterfields, and chairs were called "antimacassars" as they originated to prevent the staining caused by resting your oil-laden head.

HAIR RESTORATIVE— *To* TURN GRAY HAIR *to a* DARK COLOR

1 dram each of Lac sulphur, sugar of lead, 2 drams of muriate of soda, 2 ounces glycerine, 8 ounces bay rum, 4 ounces Jamaica rum, 1 pint soft water. Shake well before using and keep in a dark place.

REMARKS—preparations containing lead sometimes affects the muscles of the eyelids causing them to droop. I think if only used once a week, even wetting the scalp will not do this, but if the hair only is moistened it is all sufficient, not wetting the head or scalp.

DR. CHASE'S RECIPES, C. 1884

CARE *of the* HAIR

Thorough combing, washing in suds or New England rum and thorough brushing will keep it in order and the washing does not injure the hair as is generally supposed. Do not sleep with hair frizzled or braided.

THE AMERICAN FRUGAL
HOUSEWIFE, 1832

BALDNESS

If a young lady's hair is coming out then try rubbing paraffin into the skin of your head. If the hair that is falling out is square at the end you need not be alarmed about the loss of your hair; if, however, it is pointed, that is, if the hair which comes out is fresh hair and has never been cut, then it is serious and you ought to consult some reliable hair doctor at once.

And:

To
ENCOURAGE
HAIR GROWTH

The very best way of making the hair grow is to rub paraffin into the roots but, of course, you must be very careful afterwards not to go near a fire or light of any kind. The next best cure is to rub the head with vaseline.

THE GIRL'S OWN ANNUAL,

VOL. XXIV, 1903

Ed. Note: Here is a very dangerous hair tonic containing lead.

HAIR TONIC

One half ounce sugar of lead, one half ounce of lac sulphur, one quart of rose water, six tablespoons castor oil.

THE CANADIAN HOME
COOK BOOK, 1877

HAIR SHOULD NEVER BE WASHED IN HARD WATER. This is the cause of much of the prevalent baldness.

THE GIRL'S OWN ANNUAL,
VOL. XXVII, 1907

HAIR DYES

One of the European journals relates the case of a gentleman who became a maniac in consequence of the free use of a hair dye. We know of no efficient hair dye which does not owe its prompt virtues to a solution of "nitrate of silver" which, in its solid state, is known by the name of "lunar caustic"; it stains the skin black by burning it and will burn into the flesh if steadily applied.

Hair dyes for whiskers have become very common of late years, they have to be repeated once a month. Their more immediate effect is to impart a dead black color, which at once reveals the hypocrisy and that it should so disturb the natural functions of the skin by such frequent application as to lay the foundation for callosities, cancers and other affections.

THE GUIDE BOARD
TO HEALTH, PEACE AND
COMPETENCE, 1869

Ed. Note: With the inclusion of arsenic, this could be a deadly method of removing unwanted hair.

To

DESTROY SUPERFLUOUS HAIR

Take 1 ounce of fresh stone lime, 1 dram pure potash, 1 dram sulphuret of arsenic. Directions—Reduce them to a fine powder in an earthen or glass mortar and add enough soft water to make a thin paste. Then wash the hair in warm water and apply the paste by rubbing gently a little on the spot where you wish to remove the hair. As soon as the skin is much reddened, wash it off with strong vinegar. Do not let it remain on more than 3 to 5 minutes. Wash the place with a flannel cloth and the hair will be removed.

DR. CHASE'S RECIPES,
c. 1884

"BEWARE

OF A

POOR VOICE

IN YOUR

BRIDE"

MORALS,

MARRIAGE,

AND

GOOD LIVING

The CAYENNE CURE for ALCOHOLISM

The remarkable success which has attended the use of Cayenne as a substitute for alcohol with hard drinkers and as a valuable drug in delirium tremens, has led physicians to regard the Cayenne (Capsicum) as a highly useful, stimulating and restorative medicine. For an intemperate person who really desires to wean himself from spirituous liquors and yet feels the need of a substitute at first, a mixture of tincture of Capsicum with tincture of orange peel and water will answer very effectually, the doses being reduced in strength and frequency from day to day. In delirium tremens, if the tincture of Capsicum be given in doses of half a drachm well diluted with water, it will reduce the tremor and agitation in a few hours, inducing presently a calm prolonged sleep.

HERBAL SIMPLES, 1914

A WOMAN SHOULD NEVER MAKE AN ADVANCE TOWARDS THE MAN SHE LOVES AND WOULD MARRY. Such a step is deemed inconsistent with maiden modesty.

TITCOMB'S LETTERS TO YOUNG PEOPLE, 1859

LIQUOR:
A CURE *for the* LOVE *of* IT

The prescription is simply an orange every morning a half hour before breakfast.

Take that and you will neither want liquor nor medicine. The liquor will become repulsive.

**DR. CHASE'S RECIPES,
C. 1884**

DRINKING WHISKEY

Whiskey cures a great many ailments, infallibly, by killing the patient.

**FUN BETTER THAN PHYSIC,
1877**

SUMMONED TO ATTEND AN ELDERLY LADY IN A DECLINE, I OCCASIONALLY HEARD A SHOUT IN THE BACK YARD, sounding as if made by one intoxicated and, at length, saw an apparently drunken female, throwing up her hands, jumping up and shouting. I asked my patient what all this meant and she replied "she is my eldest daughter, and has always been thus, obviously because her father begot her when intoxicated, though a teetotaler at all other times."

A teetotal father, intoxicated while exhilarated, begets a besotted-appearing daughter who all her life keeps doing just what he did for an hour before she received being.

CREATIVE AND SEXUAL
SCIENCE, 1876

A very common courting custom in Colonial New England was "bundling." If a couple were "walking out together" and their farm homes very far distant, the young man might be invited to "bundle" with the young lady overnight. It must be remembered that in early Canada and America ☞

the homes were extremely small and perhaps consisted of just one or two rooms. Private bedrooms were virtually unknown and beds just stood in the main living area. A "bundling board" would be prepared. This was either, as the name implies, a straight log or a few blankets rolled up and placed down the middle of the bed.

Father might insist that the girl's legs be tied together. The young couple spent the night virtuously, getting to know one another while keeping to the straight and narrow. In later years, after the American Revolution of 1776, it was beginning to fall into social disapproval and the practice was mostly abandoned. It is also of note that premarital sex and illegitimate babies vastly increased after 1776.

> THE AGE FIXED BY LAW FOR CON-
> SENT TO MATRIMONY IS FOURTEEN
> IN MALES AND TWELVE IN FEMALES.
> CASSELL'S HOUSEHOLD
> GUIDE, C. 1880

OCCUPATIONS
of LIFE

Blondes, that is, persons with light hair, fair skin and blue eyes, as also those having sandy or reddish hair, should, by all means, select some active, outdoor vocation.

Brunettes, persons having a dark skin, indicating the bilious temperament, accompanied usually with black hair and dark eyes, should select a calling which, whether indoor or out, will require them to be on their feet, moving about nearly all the time in order to "work off" the constantly accumulating bile.

The mixed temperaments can best bear sedentary, indoor occupation; such as a combination of the bilious and nervous.

THE GUIDE BOARD
TO HEALTH, PEACE AND
COMPETENCE, 1869

CAPITAL PUNISHMENT *for* HORSE THIEVES

The best specific for a horse thief is a hempen halter. Never, since the world began, has it ever been found necessary to repeat the dose.

FUN BETTER THAN PHYSIC,
1877

> **T**HE GIRLS OF OUR COUNTRY ARE TRAINED AND EDUCATED IN THE IDEA THAT MATRIMONY IS THE END AND AIM OF THEIR EXISTENCE; to marry well, that is, to marry wealth if possible, but at all events to marry.
>
> SEXOLOGY, 1904

A
MANLY "POPPING"
of the QUESTION

Girls say "yes" to all questions "popped" in a deep rich, strong, rumbling, powerful male voice, but they say "no" to questions popped in a weak, quackling, piping, thin, squeak-mouse, gelding voice.

CREATIVE AND SEXUAL
SCIENCE, 1876

Ed. Note: I don't believe the advice given here would be tolerated for one minute today. It says nothing about the girl pointing out faults to the young man, only the reverse. He says, "frank interchange," but it is strictly one-sided.

CONDUCT
of the ENGAGED
COUPLE

It is the privilege of the betrothed lover, as it is also his duty, to give advice to the fair one who now implicitly confides in him. Should he detect a fault, should he observe failings which he would wish removed or amended, let him avail himself of this season, so favorable for the frank interchange of thought between the betrothed pair, to urge their correction. He will find a ready listener; and any judicious counsel offered to her by him will now be gratefully received and remembered in after life. After marriage it may be too late; for advice on trivial points of conduct may then not improbably be resented by the wife as an unnecessary interference; now, the fair and loving creature is disposed like pliant wax in his hands to mold herself to his reasonable wishes in all things.

COLLIER'S CYCLOPEDIA OF
SOCIAL AND COMMERCIAL
INFORMATION, 1882

SLEEPING TOGETHER

It would be a constitutional and moral good for married persons to sleep in adjoining rooms as a general habit. It would be a certain means of physical invigoration and of advantages in other directions, which will readily occur to the reflective reader. Kings and

queens and the highest personages of courts have separate apartments. It is the bodily emanations, collecting and concentrating under the same cover, which are the most destructive to health, more destructive than the simple contamination of an atmosphere breathed in common.

THE GUIDE BOARD TO
HEALTH, PEACE AND
COMPETENCE, 1869

ALL GIRLS' VOICES CHANGE AS THEY MERGE FROM GIRLHOOD INTO WOMANHOOD. Contrast the indifferent, insipid singing of all undeveloped girls with the rich, thrilling voices of the fully developed women of the choir and behold the cause of all this difference in the incipient sexuality of all girls and the complete sexual

maturity of women. But let a girl catch a hard cold soon after her monthlies commence, say at fourteen, which stops them, it thereby chills and palsies her whole sexual nature and arrests her female development and sexual growth, holding all in status quo, voice included, so this poor girl's voice remains just where it was when this cold struck her. Marriage may start up this sexual growth again but she will find herself and be found, to be ungrown sexually and quite too small for the practical purposes of marriage. To avoid wedding such would be hard on millions thus impaired and leave the great body of modern girls unmarriageable, yet save many bridegrooms, now ignorant of this fact, sad disappointment. Such girls will make poor wives.

CREATIVE AND SEXUAL
SCIENCE, 1876

CURE *for* NYMPHOMANIA

Wear a wet diaper, day and night. Wearing a wet towel on the abdomen, extending low down and between the thighs will be all the time carrying off the heat.

CREATIVE AND SEXUAL
SCIENCE, 1876

Ed. Note: Interesting to note, in the following item, that reading has not always been regarded as a healthy pastime—how contrary to our views of today when we encourage our children to pick up a book! The only books recommended in those days were edifying and pious religious works, far too heavy for young minds and ones that certainly didn't make reading enjoyable.

NOVEL READING

Novel reading produces a morbid appetite for excitement. The object of the novelist, generally, is to produce the highest possible degree of excitement, both of the mind and the passions. The object is very similar to that of intoxicating liquors on the body; hence, the confirmed novel-reader becomes a kind of literary inebriate, to whom the things of entity have no attractions and whose thirst cannot be slaked. . . .

Novel reading strengthens the passions, weakens the virtues and diminishes the power of self-control. Multitudes may date their ruin from the commencement of this kind of reading; and many more, who have been rescued from the snare, will regret, to the end of their days, its influence in the early formation of their character.

If you wish to become weak-headed, nervous and good for nothing, read novels.

THE LADIES VASE OR POLITE
MANUAL FOR YOUNG LADIES, 1847

MARRIAGE IS THE NATURAL STATE OF HUMANKIND. There never can be lasting good health without it, it is an impossibility, except combined with criminal practices. A person may live in good health to the age of twenty-five, but if marriage is deferred beyond that, every month's delay is the eating out, more and more, the very essence of life and the worm of certain disease and premature death burrows the more deeply into the vitals. On the other hand, marriage not later than twenty-five prolongs life.

FUN BETTER THAN
PHYSIC, 1877

SUCCESSFUL MEN

In reading the lives of men who have greatly distinguished themselves, we find their whole youth passed in self-denials of food, rest, sleep and recreation. They sat up late and rose early to the performance of imperative duties; doing by daylight the work of one man and, by night, the work of another. Said a gentleman, the other day, now a private banker of high integrity and whom we knew had started in life without a dollar, "for years together I was in my place of business at sunrise and often did not leave it for fifteen and eighteen hours."

Let not, therefore, any youth be discouraged, if he has to make his own living or even to support a widowed mother or sick sister or unfortunate relation; for this has been the road to eminence of many a proud name.

THE GUIDE BOARD TO
HEALTH, PEACE AND
COMPETENCE, 1869

A MAN OUT OF MONEY CANNOT BE HAPPY. A man out of health cannot be happy. A man without a wife cannot be happy. Therefore, I have come to the conclusion that the best way to be happy is to take care of your health, keep out of debt and get a wife.

THE GUIDE BOARD
TO HEALTH, PEACE AND
COMPETENCE, 1869

Down through the ages there have been many bizarre remedies for impotency. One of the first was a plant called "satyrion," tried about twenty-five hundred years ago. Hippocrates recommended deer genitals and these were used as recently as the eighteenth century. A few other tonics and remedies in folklore are seal genitals, absinthe, black ants, lizards, snake's blood, fat from a camel's hump, the king eider goose down, gingko, shark fins, ambergris, reindeer antlers, rhino horns, gallstones from animals, toad skin, soup made from a tiger's penis, and oysters (Casanova was reputed to eat fifty every morning). Looks like Viagra has finally solved this universal problem.

YOUNG   LADIES   YOU   WILL
NEVER   BE   SATISFIED   UNTIL   YOU
[GET MARRIED]! It is the surest road to
a long life and a happy one. There is a thorn
in the path now and then but there is a rose
always hard by. The roses
and the thorns of mar-
ried life are not one
and indivisible, they
grow on separate stocks
and all that is required to
part them is a good head and a
kind heart. There is one difficulty in the
way; the thorns are indestructible, but you
have only to throw them aside and if any-
body else chooses to pick them that is their
lookout, every one must see for himself.

A bunch of this sort happened to fall to
our lot once upon a time but we can easily
account for it and that is highly satisfactory,
we always had weak eyes, and the vicinage

thereof is much of a sameness, in a certain phase of the moon. But we fully calculate on repeating the operation; and we intend to have a pair of specs, next time, such as will diminish the blinding glare which curls and cottons, in certain conjunctions, attitudes and combinations do most devastatingly throw around them.

THE GUIDE BOARD
TO HEALTH, PEACE AND
COMPETENCE, 1869

"BAKE YOUR

QUILT IN THE

OVEN"

AND

OTHER HORRIBLE

HOUSEHOLD

HINTS

EGGS—*To* KEEP NINE MONTHS

To 4 gallons of boiling water add ½ peck of new lime, stirring it some little time. When cold remove any hard lumps there may be with a sieve, add 10 ounces of salt, 3 ounces of cream of tartar and mix thoroughly. The mixture should stand a fortnight before using. The eggs to be packed as closely as possible and be closely covered up. New laid eggs may be kept 9 months using this method.

DR. CHASE'S RECIPES,

C. 1884

FRUIT SHOULD BE EATEN RIPE, RAW, FRESH AND PERFECT. It should be eaten in moderation. It should be eaten not later than four o'clock in the afternoon.

No water, or fluid of any description, should be swallowed within an hour after eating fruit.

THE GUIDE BOARD
TO HEALTH, PEACE AND
COMPETENCE, 1869

To
WASH CARPETS

Spread the carpet where you can use a brush; take Irish potatoes and scrape them into a pail or tub of water and let them stand overnight, using one peck to clean a large carpet; two pails of water is sufficient to let them stand in, and you can add more when ready to use; add two ounces of beef gall and use with a brush, as to scrub a floor; the particles of potato will help cleanse. When dry, brush with a broom or stiff brush.

THE CANADIAN HOME
COOK BOOK, 1877

RATS—*To* GET RID *of* *without* POISON, GERMAN METHOD

A German paper gives the following plan of doing this: Having first for some days placed pieces of cheese in a part of the premises so as to induce the rats to come in great numbers to their accustomed feeding-place, a piece of cheese is fixed on a fish-hook about a foot above the floor. One rat leaps at this and, of course, remains suspended. Hereafter all the other rats take sudden flight and at once quit the house in a body.

DR. CHASE'S RECIPES,
c. 1884

Ed. Note: This is appalling, but quite an amusing bit of advice.

To RID YOUR HOUSE of COCKROACHES

Let your wife finish making peach preserves late at night in a smooth, bright, brass kettle; then persuade her it is too late to clean the kettle till morning, but set it against the wall where the insects are thickest and retire to rest. In the morning you will find the sides of the kettle bright as a new dollar but you will find every insect that was hungry in the bottom of the kettle. Then treat them to a sufficient quantity of boiling water to render them perfectly harmless. As I thought molasses cheaper than peach preserve juice, I ever afterward baited the same trap with molasses and I caught the last one of millions.

DR. CHASE'S RECIPES,
C. 1884

Ed. Note: How different from our present thoughts on how to beautify your surroundings.

IT LOOKS WELL IN THE MIDST OF SUMMER TO SEE A TIDY FARMHOUSE ALMOST HIDDEN FROM VIEW BY TREES AND BUSHES; but the influence they have in keeping a dwelling damp in summer and in producing a raw and chilly atmosphere in winter, thus engendering disease the year round, are sufficient reasons for exercising a wise discretion in this direction. Have neither tree nor bush within twenty or thirty feet of the front of the farmhouse unless it be a flowering plant here and there.

THE GUIDE BOARD TO HEALTH, PEACE AND COMPETENCE, 1869

AFTER BREAKFAST

After breakfast is over, it will be well for the mistress to make a round of the kitchen and other offices, to see that all are in order and that the morning's work has been properly performed by the various domestics. The orders for the day should then be given and any questions which the domestics desire to ask, respecting their several departments, should be answered and any special articles they may require handed to them from the store closet.

MRS. BEETON'S BOOK OF
HOUSEHOLD MANAGEMENT, 1861

MOTHS *in a* DOWN QUILT

The best way to get rid of the moths in your down quilt is to bake it in an oven.

THE GIRL'S OWN ANNUAL,
VOL. XXIV, 1903

Ed. Note: To save the housewife a few precious pennies, there was packaged "tea-dust" for sale in the grocery shops.

TEA

Tea-dust professes to be simply the broken tea taken from the bottom of the chest or made in packing, is as good as the unbroken leaf, but it is very frequently the sweepings of warehouses, mixed with dirt and therefore not always a desirable article to use. Many of the "cheap" teas are also adulterated, sometimes by the Chinese and sometimes in this country. Tea

leaves which have been already used are, in some cases, manipulated and sold for the genuine article and occasionally the leaves of other plants are added to those of the tea plant.

BEETON'S SIXPENNY COOKERY
BOOK FOR THE PEOPLE, C. 1890

COLD WATER IS INJURIOUS TO HEALTH IF TAKEN AT MEALS. Injurious to the most robust if taken largely; and to persons in a feeble health, if taken at all, beyond a few swallows, at a meal. I therefore set it down as a clearly established fact, that a glass or more of cold water, drank habitually at meals or soon after, is a pernicious practice, even to the most healthy.

THE GUIDE BOARD
TO HEALTH, PEACE AND
COMPETENCE, 1869

Ed. Note: This next recipe is almost incomprehensible to us today. Can you imagine the odor of melting rubber boots on the stove? Pity the poverty that drove people to such desperate measures! In Britain these boots are called "Wellingtons." The Duke of Wellington started the fad.

RUBBER
WATER-PROOFING
for BOOTS

Two pounds of old rubber boots. 1 pint Neat's-foot oil, 1 oz. Rosin. Directions: Melt slowly (all together) and then pour off from or take out the cloth of the old boots and apply warm. The boots will be water and snow-proof.

DR. CHASE'S RECIPES, C. 1884

Ed. Note: "Neat" is an alternative word for an ox or a cow.

WHILE PLANTS CONTAIN A LARGE AMOUNT OF MATERIAL WHICH CANNOT BE DIGESTED AND ARE HENCE WORTHLESS AS FOOD, yet because of the starch and sugar which they contain, vegetables are fattening food. This was well understood by Mr. Banting, who devised the famous method which bears his name, for reducing the flesh.

THE PRACTICAL HOME PHYSICIAN, 1892

Ed. Note: This is a simply dreadful piece of advice rather smugly passed on by a farmer. An archaeologist in the future will have a field day when he comes to this well. Just think of the danger of all that strychnine being spread around!

SHEEP *vs.* DOGS— HOW *to* GIVE *the* ADVANTAGE *to* SHEEP

I keep my sheep yarded nights and I go out at bedtime and place around the outside of the pen bits of meat containing strychnine, which I take up again early in the morning if not

eaten during the night. Result, immunity from dogs and an old well on the farm has received a layer of dogs and a layer of dirt until it is about full.

DR. CHASE'S RECIPES,
C. 1884

MILK

Many persons imagine that the milk of cows is one of the most healthful of all articles, and yet it is a great mistake, except under certain limitations. By stout, strong, hardy, industrious out-door working men it may be used advantageously for breakfast and dinner, but, except in tea and coffee, and now and then half a glass for breakfast or dinner, it is not a proper article of food for invalids.

THE GUIDE BOARD TO
HEALTH, PEACE AND
COMPETENCE, 1869

PURIFYING DRINKING WATER

Pulverized alum possesses the property of purifying water. A large spoonful stirred into a hogshead of water will so purify it that, in a few hours, the dirt will all sink to the bottom and it will be as fresh and clear as spring water. Four gallons may be purified by a teaspoonful.

THE AMERICAN FRUGAL
HOUSEWIFE, 1832

Ed. Note: I certainly would not want to drink of this water! This was probably rainwater collected in a barrel, a fine catchall for insects, dead frogs, and other debris!

Ed. Note: One explanation of why baths were only taken on Saturday nights.

A
CLOSE SUPPLY
of WATER

There are thousands of farms in this country where the spring which supplies all the water, for drink and cooking, is from a quarter to

more than half a mile distant from the house and a "pailful" is brought at a time, involving five or ten miles' walking in a day, for months and years together; when a man in half a day could make a slide, and with a fifty-cent barrel could, in half an hour, deliver at the door, enough to last the whole day.

THE GUIDE BOARD TO HEALTH,
PEACE AND COMPETENCE, 1869

HOW *to* MAKE SOAP

All fat and grease from the kitchen should be carefully saved and should be made into soap before accumulating and becoming offensive. Boil for six hours ten gallons of lye made of green wood ashes. Then add eight or ten pounds of grease and continue to boil it. If thick or ropy, add more lye.

HOUSEKEEPING IN
OLD VIRGINIA, 1879

WASHING *is* HARD WORK!

No farmer's wife, who is a mother, ought to be allowed to do the washing of the family; it is perilous to any woman who has not a vigorous constitution.

THE GUIDE BOARD TO HEALTH, PEACE AND COMPETENCE, 1869

CLEANING POTS, KETTLES *and* TINS

Boil a double handful of hay or grass in a new iron pot before attempting to cook with it; scrub it out with soap and sand then set on full

A THUNDER-STORM WILL TURN THE MILK: THIS ELECTRICAL INFLUENCE GIVES THE MILK AN ACID REACTION AND RENDERS IT UNFIT FOR USE.

SEXOLOGY, 1904

Ed. Note: We know now that it is the humid weather associated with summer thunderstorms that causes the milk to sour.

of fair water and let it boil half an hour. After this you may use it without fear. New tins should stand near the fire with boiling water in them, in which has been dissolved a spoonful of soda, for an hour then be scoured inside with soft soap; afterward rinsed with hot water. Keep them clean by rubbing with sifted wood ashes or whitening. Copper utensils should be cleaned with brickdust and flannel.

THE GIRL'S OWN ANNUAL, VOL. XXIV, 1903

In the larger cities of Great Britain in Victorian times, if you were lucky, you might have a "wash house" located near your dwelling. These were located in the back courtyards of tenement buildings. The public ones contained baths for your weekly scrub-down and the "steamy" where you did your laundry. They were run either by the local council or as private businesses. These were still in common use right up to the beginning of World ☞

War II. The necessity for these wash houses becomes evident when you consider that most of the population lived in squalor, in tenement houses in the big cities. It was not at all unusual for six families to occupy a six-room house, with Mother and Father and perhaps all their children living in one room, and doing all their cooking and sleeping in there, too. How, then, could the housewife do the laundry and where would it be hung to dry? The wash house was a marvelous and modern convenience!

In rural North America the water usually had to be fetched from a nearby stream or, if you were lucky, from the well near your home. It would be carried and poured into an enormous pot over an open fire. In Britain it was called "the copper." No one had hot water "on tap."

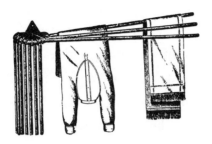

The fire was located either in the farmyard or in the "summer kitchen" at the back of the house.

Washing the clothes was only a small part of laundry day; in those days there was also a process called "bluing," which some of my older readers may remember. Little blocks of special blue dye were sold and dissolved in the final rinse water to make linens and clothing "whiter than white." Then there was the starching of the shirts, pillowcases, blouses, etc.

After the clothes had dried on the line they had to be sprinkled ☞

with water and rolled up to make them uniformly damp and ready to be ironed. With no electric irons, the big old flat irons or crimping irons had to be heated either on the stove or over an open fire. What a tedious job! Larger articles were mangled. Wealthy households owned their own mangle, which was like a large and heavy wringer used to smooth out the wrinkles. Men's shirts had detachable collars and these could be laundered without having to wash the entire shirt.

Because of all these difficulties, laundry was postponed until it was absolutely necessary. There were special menus for washing day because if a wife had to do her own laundry, it was too much to expect that she could also prepare a hot dinner for the family.

MATTRESS STUFFINGS

Barley straw is the best for beds; dry corn-husks, slit into shreds, are far better than straw. Straw beds are much better for being boxed at the sides; in the same manner upholsterers prepare ticks for feathers.

THE AMERICAN FRUGAL
HOUSEWIFE, 1832

Ed. Note: As a horrible example of how our ancestors overcooked their veggies, consider this next recipe where green beans are cooked for a total of three hours. All that work, and the nourishment would be completely gone. Today we'd give them about three or four minutes!

CANNED STRING
BEANS

String and break, cover with hot water and cook two hours. Fill glass jars full of beans

> **S**OME OF THE MOST TERRIBLE
> FORMS OF DISEASE ARE BROUGHT ON
> BY PERSISTENCE IN EATING COLD FOOD.
>
> THE GUIDE BOARD
> TO HEALTH, PEACE AND
> COMPETENCE, 1869

with the water they have been cooking in, place rubbers and covers on, screw nearly tight and cook one hour longer in a kettle of hot water, tighten covers, wrap in paper and keep in a cool dark place.

OGILVIE'S BOOK
FOR A COOK, 1909

A PARTY OF MEN LEFT SALT LAKE CITY FOR ST. LOUIS WITH THE UNITED STATES MAIL TO BE DELIVERED AT INDEPENDENCE OR "ST. JO." It was winter. They found the prairies covered with snow and finally their animals perished with hunger; at this stage the six men found themselves utterly destitute of any kind of food; the game had taken to the woods, there were no rivers and they were still hundreds of miles from their journey's end while the bleak winter winds whistling across the wide prairies in unobstructed fury, froze them sometimes almost to the heart's core. All, absolutely all, they had to subsist upon under these desperate conditions was snow-water and a quantity of green coffee; this they burned and boiled in snow-water and upon it traveled for six days until they reached a place of help. These are the bare facts of the case as reported to the government, and demonstrate that coffee alone is a sustenant as well as a stimulant. That it contains the elements of nutrition. Coffee, then, being of itself nutritious, capable of sustaining life for days at a time, the conclusion appears to us as legitimate as one of Euclid's corollaries, that coffee as generally used in this country, is a valuable, nutritious, healthful and comfortable item.

Chemical analysis has, of late, under the direction of the most competent and intelligent minds of the age, arrived at the point just stated and declares that coffee is a nutriment.

THE GUIDE BOARD TO HEALTH,
PEACE AND COMPETENCE, 1869

"TONGUE TOAST"

AND

OTHER

REVOLTING

RECIPES

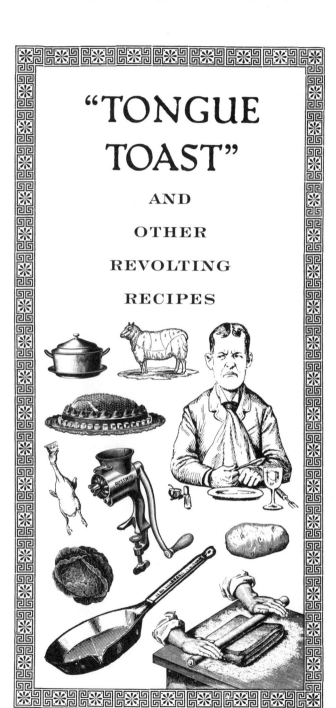

To BROIL ROBINS and OTHER SMALL BIRDS

They should be carefully cleaned, buttered, sprinkled with pepper and salt and broiled. When they are served, butter them again. If you like, serve each bird on a piece of toast and pour over them a sauce of red wine, mushroom, catsup, salt, cayenne pepper and celery.

HOUSEKEEPING IN
OLD VIRGINIA, 1879

Ed. Note: Our American robin is the bird referred to above—misnamed by early settlers, for it is actually a thrush. The English robin is a very tiny bird and you'd have trouble broiling enough to feed anyone—but not for want of trying! Small songbirds are considered a delicacy in Italy and France, where they catch them by using nets. There has been some outcry by naturalists against this practice as some species are now seriously endangered.

To
COOK FROGS

As potpies, stews and chowder they are a failure. The only legitimate way to cook a frog is to fry him brown in sweet table butter. As a preliminary he must be dipped in a batter of cracker dust, which should adhere closely when cooked forming a dainty cracknel of a golden brown color, with a crisp tang to it when submitted to the teeth. The tender juices thus retained lose none of their delicate flavor and the dainty morsel needs no condiments to give it an additional zest. Next to the pleasure of sitting on the borders of a frog-pond at eventide and listening to their sweet, melancholy *ch-r-r-rk* is that of reviewing a plate heaped high with the mementoes of a finished feast—the bones of the "Frog that would a wooing go" and a goodly portion of his kindred. Having eaten them done thusly, I can say try them every chance you can get. They are splendid.

DR. CHASE'S RECIPES,
C. 1884

RATTLESNAKE

In some parts of North America the Indians broil rattlesnake like eels and eat them. Their flesh is said to be white and delicate. When the

rattlesnake is asleep they fix him to the ground and, by inducing him to fasten his fangs in a piece of leather, they pluck out the poison-fangs by pulling away the leather. They then in safety take off the skin and broil the flesh.

DICTIONARY OF COOKERY,
1899

ROOK PIE

Skin and draw six young rooks and cut out the backbones. Season them with pepper and salt, put them in a deep dish with half a pint of water, lay some bits of butter over them and cover the dish with a tolerably thick crust. Let the pie be well baked.

DICTIONARY OF COOKERY,
1899

Ed. Note: A rook is a wild blackbird very similar to a crow. I believe these were the "four and twenty blackbirds" in the nursery rhyme "Sing a Song of Sixpence."

SQUIRRELS

The large gray squirrel is seldom eaten at the North, but in great request in Virginia and other Southern States. It is generally barbecued, precisely as are rabbits; broiled, fricasseed or, most popular of all, made into a Brunswick stew. This is named from Brunswick County, Virginia and is a famous dish, or was, at the political and social pic-nics known as barbecues.

BRUNSWICK STEW

2 squirrels — 3, if small,

1 quart of tomatoes, peeled and sliced

1 pint butter beans or lima beans

6 potatoes, parboiled and sliced

6 ears of green corn cut from the cob

½ lb. butter

½ lb. fat salt pork

1 teaspoonful ground black pepper

Half a teaspoonful cayenne

1 gallon water,

1 tablespoonful salt

2 teaspoonsful white sugar
1 onion, minced small

Put on the water with the salt in it and boil five minutes. Put in the onion, beans, corn, pork or bacon cut into shreds, potatoes, pepper and the squirrels which must first be cut into joints and laid in cold water and salt to draw out the blood. Cover closely and stew two and a half hours very slowly, stirring frequently from the bottom. Then add the tomatoes and sugar and stew an hour longer. Ten minutes before you take it from the fire add the butter, cut into bits the size of a walnut, rolled in flour. Give a final boil, taste to see that it is seasoned to your liking and turn into a soup tureen. It is eaten from soup plates. Chickens may be substituted for squirrels.

COMMON SENSE IN THE
HOUSEHOLD, 1871

PIGEON PIE

Take six young pigeons. After they are drawn, trussed and singed, stuff them with the chopped livers mixed with parsley, salt, pepper and a small piece of butter. Cover the bottom of the dish with rather small pieces of beef. On the beef, place a thin layer of chopped

parsley and mushrooms, seasoned with pepper and salt. Over this place the pigeons, between each putting the yolk of a hard-boiled egg. Add some brown sauce or gravy.

Cover with puff paste and bake the pie for an hour and a half.

HOUSEKEEPING IN
OLD VIRGINIA, 1879

SWEETBREAD
of HOG

This nice morsel is between the maw and ruffle piece inside of the hog. Put them in soak for a day; parboil them and then gash them and stew them in pepper, butter, one teacup of milk and a little vinegar. Or they are very nice fried or broiled.

HOUSEKEEPING IN
OLD VIRGINIA, 1879

Ed. Note: Sweetbreads are the name for the pancreas or the thymus gland of animals. Some people thought sweetbreads were the animal's testicles; no, when these are rescued and cooked they are called "fries."

Ed. Note: The following dish is often called "head cheese" or "brawn" and can still be bought today. Such labor went into making even the simplest of luncheon meats.

Souse is a very old word meaning the brine in which meat is preserved. It is now also used to signify the pieces of pork, such as the feet and ears, which were commonly "soused."

SOUSE CHEESE

Lay the meat in cold water as cut from the hog. Let it stand three or four days, shifting the water each day. Scrape it and let it stand a day or two longer, changing the water often, and if it should turn warm, pour a little salt in the water. The oftener it is scraped, the whiter

will be the souse. Boil in plenty of water to cover it, replenishing when needed. When tender enough, put it in milk-warm water and when cold in salt water. Boil the head until the bones will almost fall out. Clean one dozen or more ears and boil also; while hot, chop very fine and season with pepper and salt.

Put in a mold or bowl with a weight on top. The feet may be soused whole or cut up with the head and ears; but it is not so nice. Clean them by dipping in boiling water and scraping; do not hold them to the fire to singe off the hair. One head and one dozen ears will make a good-sized cheese.

HOUSEKEEPING IN
OLD VIRGINIA, 1879

TONGUE TOAST

Take cold tongue that has been well boiled, mince fine, mix it well with cream or a little milk, if there is no cream. Add the beaten yolk of one egg and give it a simmer over the fire. Toast nicely some thin slices of stale bread and, having buttered, lay them in a flat dish that has been heated, then cover the toast with the tongue and serve up directly.

HOUSEKEEPING IN
OLD VIRGINIA, 1879

Ed. Note: Beef tongue was always considered a great delicacy and was usually saved as a treat for

Christmas. You could jelly it or just cook and slice it for sandwiches.

To ROAST an OX HEART

Wash it well and clean all the blood carefully from the pipes; parboil it ten or fifteen minutes in boiling water; drain and put in a stuffing which has been made of bread crumbs, minced suet or butter, thyme or parsley, salt, pepper and nutmeg. Put it down to roast while hot, baste it well with butter and just before serving, stir one tablespoonful currant jelly into the gravy. To roast allow twenty minutes to every pound.

HOUSEKEEPING IN
OLD VIRGINIA, 1879

To
DRESS BRAINS

Lay in salt and water then either scramble like eggs, or beat the yolks of eggs with a little flour; dip the brains in and fry them.

HOUSEKEEPING IN
OLD VIRGINIA, 1879

To
STEW BRAINS

Have them thoroughly soaked in salt water to get the blood out. Put them in a stewpan with water enough to cover them; boil half an hour, pour off the water and add one teacup of cream or milk, salt, pepper and butter the size of an egg. Boil well together for ten minutes, when put into the dish. Add one tablespoonful vinegar.

HOUSEKEEPING IN
OLD VIRGINIA, 1879

To

PREPARE TRIPE

Empty the contents of the stomach of a fat beef; put it in boiling water, one piece at a time to prevent getting too hot. Scrape with a sharp knife, then put it in a vessel of cold water with salt; wash thoroughly and change the salt water every day for four or five consecutive days; when perfectly white, boil in a very clean vessel of salt water. Then put it in vinegar until you wish to use it. Cut it in pieces of three or four inches square and fry in egg batter.

HOUSEKEEPING IN
OLD VIRGINIA, 1879

TURTLE SOUP

Kill the turtle at daylight in summer, the night before in winter, and hang it up to bleed. After breakfast, scald it well and scrape the outer skin off the shell; open it carefully, so as not to break the gall. Break both shells to pieces and put them into the pot. Lay the fins, the eggs and some of the more delicate parts by—put the rest into the pot with a quantity of water to suit the size of your family.

Add two onions, parsley, thyme, salt, pepper, cloves and allspice to suit your taste.

About half an hour before dinner thicken the soup with brown flour and butter rubbed together. An hour before dinner, take the parts laid by, roll them in brown flour, fry them in butter, put them and the eggs in the soup, just before dinner add a glass of claret or Madeira wine.

HOUSEKEEPING IN
OLD VIRGINIA, 1879

PIGEONS
TRANSMOGRIFIED

Pick and clean six small young pigeons but do not cut off their heads, cut off their pinions and boil them ten minutes in water, then cut off the ends of six large cucumbers and scrape out the seeds, put in your pigeons, but let the

heads be out at the ends of the cucumbers and stick a bunch of barberries in their bills and then put them in a tossing pan with a pint of veal gravy, a little anchovy, a glass of red wine, a spoonful of browning, a little slice of lemon, Cayenne and salt to your taste, stew them seven minutes, take them out, thicken your gravy with a little butter rolled in flour, boil it up and strain it over your pigeons and serve them up.

THE EXPERIENCED ENGLISH
HOUSEKEEPER, 1805

Ed. Note: "Pinions" are the ends of the wings or the wings themselves.

So, what's for dinner tonight, honey? Even reading the recipe will make you tired! This makes three different dishes for a dinner party— the "bottom dish," the "corner dish," and the "top dish." Tables were described as having "side dishes," "top dishes," etc. It is an extremely complicated recipe and would require much assistance, from other servants, in the preparation. I'm sure the cook would be up all night just preparing this dish and, when you think of it, there would be many other delicacies to prepare for the evening's repast—soups, vegetables, side dishes, a variety of desserts. To say nothing of preparing breakfast and lunch for the same day!

TO DRESS A TURTLE OF
A HUNDRED WEIGHT

Cut off the head, take care of the blood and take off all the fins, lay them in salt and water, cut off the bottom shell, then cut off the meat that grows to it. Take out the hearts, livers and lights and put them by themselves, take the bones and the flesh out of the back shell, cut the fleshy part into pieces, about two inches square, but leave the fat part which looks green and rub it first with salt and wash it in several waters to make it come clean, then put in the pieces that you took out, with three bottles of Madeira wine and four quarts of strong veal gravy, a lemon cut in slices, a bundle of sweet herbs,

a teaspoonful of cayenne, six
anchovies washed and picked clean,
a quarter of a pound of beaten mace,
a teaspoonful of mushroom powder
and half a pint of essence of ham,
[*Note: this is the only reference
I've come across for "essence of ham"—
it does sound appetizing!*] if you have
it, lay over it a coarse paste, set it
in the oven for three hours; when
it comes out take off the lid and
scum off the fat and brown it with
a salamander.

This is the bottom dish.

Then blanch the fins, cut them
off at the first joint, fry the first pinions a fine brown and put them into a
tossing pan with two quarts of strong
brown gravy, a glass of red wine and
the blood of the turtle, a large spoonful of lemon pickle, the same of
browning, two spoonfuls of mushroom catchup, cayenne and salt,

an onion stuck with cloves and a
bunch of sweet herbs; a little before
it is enough, put in an ounce of
morels, the same of truffles, stew
them gently over a slow fire for two
hours; when they are tender put
them into another tossing pan, thick-
en your gravy with flour and butter
and strain it upon them, give them
a boil and serve them up.

This is a corner dish.

Then take the thick or large part
of the fins, blanch them in warm
water and put them in a tossing pan
with three quarts of strong veal gravy,
a pint of Madeira wine, half a teaspoonful of cayenne, a little salt, half
a lemon, a little beaten mace, a teaspoonful of mushroom powder and
a bunch of sweet herbs; let them stew
until quite tender, they will take two
hours at least, then take them up into
another tossing pan, strain your ☞

gravy and make it pretty thick
with flour and butter, then put in
a few boiled force-meat balls, which
must be made of the veally part of
your turtle, left out for that purpose;
one pint of fresh mushrooms, if you
cannot get them, pickled ones will
do, and eight artichoke bottoms
boiled tender and cut in quarters;
shake them over the fire five or six
minutes, then put in half a pint of
thick cream with the yolks of six eggs
beaten exceedingly well, shake it over
the fire again till it looks thick and
white but do not let it boil; dish up
your fins with the balls, mushrooms
and artichoke bottoms over and
round them.

This is the top dish.

THE EXPERIENCED
ENGLISH HOUSEKEEPER,
1805

RABBIT PIE

Cut the rabbit into neat pieces and let them lie in lukewarm water a few minutes. Dry them and fry them for a few minutes in hot fat. Drain the pieces and lay them in a pie dish with a few slices of bacon. Cold bacon left from breakfast will do. Season nicely with salt, pepper and mace, a little minced onion may be added if liked. Barely cover the meat with warm  stock or water. Make a cover of good paste, lay it over the pie and bake an hour and a half.

BEETON'S SIXPENNY
COOKERY BOOK FOR
THE PEOPLE, C. 1890

Ed. Note: You'll notice that eggshells are included in the ingredients for this next recipe; they clarified the jelly.

LEMON JELLY

The white and shells of two eggs, the thin rind and juice of two lemons, one and a half pints of water, two ounces of amber sheet gelatine, five to six ounces of loaf sugar and one inch cinnamon, four or five cloves. Put all the ingredients into a saucepan to warm, except the eggs. Whisk the shells and whites together and add to the other ingredients. Whisk until the jelly begins to come up. Let it boil twice to clear it and then let it stand in a warm place for twenty minutes. Put through a scalded cloth or a jelly-bag three or four times or until quite clear and then put into a mould to set.

THE GIRL'S OWN ANNUAL,
VOL. XXVII, 1907

For a

NUTRITIOUS
JELLY

Lay six shanks of mutton, previously well soaked and washed, in a saucepan with a little whole black pepper, a blade of mace and half an onion; a crust of bread well toasted. Add three pints of water. Put the saucepan on the fire and let it simmer gently for three or four hours. Strain off and set by to cool. This dish may be improved by adding half a pound of beef. Sheep's trotters may be cooked in a similar manner. When cold, take off the fat. Warm up when required.

BEETON'S SIXPENNY COOKERY BOOK
FOR THE PEOPLE, c. 1890

Ed. Note: For poorer families there was absolutely nothing wasted.

PIG'S EARS

Pig's ears are generally dressed with the feet. They may, however, be stuffed and stewed as follows: bone an anchovy and pound it to a paste. Mix with it six ounces of grated bread crumbs, two ounces of minced veal, four ounces of shredded suet, a teaspoonful of shredded parsley and two or three sage leaves. Season this force-meat with salt and cayenne and bind it together with the yolks of two eggs. Take two or four ears which have been already soaked for some hours and partially boiled. Raise the skin of the upper side and fill them with the stuffing. Fry them in hot fat till they are brightly browned, drain them well and stew them gently in three quarters of a pint of very rich brown gravy, nicely flavored and highly seasoned. Serve the ears on a hot dish with the gravy strained and poured round them. If liked, a puree of peas can be sent to the table with them.

DICTIONARY OF COOKERY, 1899

Ed. Note: Oh, how they did overcook their veggies in those days.

COOKING VEGETABLES

Cabbages need to be boiled an hour. Beets an hour and a half. Parsnips should boil an hour or an hour and a quarter, according to size. Asparagus should be boiled fifteen or twenty minutes or half an hour, if old. Green peas should be boiled from twenty minutes to sixty. String beans the same, according to their age. Corn should be boiled from twenty minutes to forty, according to age. Dandelions half an hour or three quarters. Beet tops should be boiled twenty minutes and spinage three or four minutes.

THE AMERICAN
FRUGAL HOUSEWIFE,
1832

SELECT BIBLIOGRAPHY

An American Lady. *The Ladies Vase or Polite Manual for Young Ladies.* 3rd ed. Hartford: Henry S. Parsons, 1847.

The Bazar Book of Decorum. New York: Harper & Brothers, 1870.

Beeton, Isabella. *Beeton's Sixpenny Cookery Book for the People and Housekeeper's Guide to Comfort, Economy and Health.* London: Ward Lock & Co., c. 1890.

Beeton, Isabella. *Dictionary of Cookery.* 1899.

Beeton, Isabella. *Mrs. Beeton's Book of Household Management.* 1st ed. London: Ward, Lock & Co., 1861.

The Canadian Home Cook Book. Compiled by the Ladies of Toronto and Chief Cities and Towns in Canada. Toronto: Hunter, Rose and Company, 1877.

Cassell's Household Guide, Vols. 1 and 2. London: Cassell, Petter and Galpin, c. 1880.

Chase, A. W. *Dr. Chase's Recipes, or, Information for Everybody.* Ann Arbor: Chase, 1866.

Child, Lydia Marie. *The American Frugal Housewife.* Boston: Carter & Hendee, 1832.

Child, Lydia Marie. *The Family Nurse.* Boston: Charles J. Hendee, 1837.

Collier's Cyclopedia of Social and Commercial Information. Compiled by Nugent Robinson. New York: P. F. Collier, 1882.

Cooke, Nicolas F. *Satan in Society.* New York: C. F. Vent, 1871.

Cooper, J. W. *The Experienced Botanist or Indian Physician, being a New System of Practice founded on Botany.* Lancaster, 1840.

Fernie, W. T., M.D. *Herbal Simples.* 3rd ed. Bristol: John Wright & Sons, Ltd., 1914.

Fowler, O. S. *Creative and Sexual Science.* New Burnswick: Thompson & Company General Agents, 1876.

The Girl's Own Annual. Vol. 24. London, 1903.

The Girl's Own Annual. Vol. 27. London, 1907.

Hall, Florence Howe. *Social Customs.* Boston: Dana Estes & Co., 1911.

Hall, W. W., M.D. *Fun Better Than Physic or Everybody's Life Preserver.* Springfield: D. E. Fisk and Company, 1877.

Hall, W. W., M.D. *The Guide Board to Health, Peace and Competence.* Springfield: D. E. Fisk & Co., 1869.

Harland, Marion. *Common Sense in the Household.* New York: Charles Scribner & Co., 1871.

Ladies' Indispensable Assistant. New York: E. Hutchinson, 1851.

Lyman, Henry et al., *The Practical Home Physician.* Ontario: World Publishing Company, 1892.

Mather, W. *The Young Man's Companion.* London, 1775.

Napheys, Geo. H., A.M. M.D. *The Physical Life of Woman—Advice to the Maiden, Wife and Mother.* Philadelphia: George Maclean, 1872.

Ogilvie's Book for a Cook. Montreal: Ogilvie Flour Mills Company Ltd., 1909.

Raffald, Elizabeth. *The Experienced English Housekeeper, For the Use and Ease of Ladies, Housekeepers, Cooks, &c. Written purely from practice; Dedicated to the Hon. Lady Elizabeth Warburton, Whom the Author lately served as Housekeeper.* London: H. Mozley, 1805.

Titcomb, Timothy. *Titcomb's Letters to Young People.* 15th ed. New York: Charles Scribner, 1859.

Tyree, Marion Fontaine Cabell. *Housekeeping in Old Virginia.* Richmond: J.W. Randolph & English, 1878.

Walling, William H., A.M. M.D. *Sexology.* Philadelphia: Puritan Publishing, 1904.